W9-BRX-343

LIVING WITH MATH

MAKING HEALTHY DECISIONS
FOR YOURSELF AND THE EARTH

George,
Hope you
enjoy it.
As always

Ira

✳✳✳✳✳✳✳✳

LIVING WITH MATH

MAKING HEALTHY DECISIONS
FOR YOURSELF AND THE EARTH

✳✳✳✳✳✳✳✳

IRA NIRENBERG

 Pi Press

Copyright © 1997 by Ira Nirenberg
All rights reserved

Printed in the United States of America

Library of Congress Number: 96-85805
Nirenberg, Ira
    Living With Math: Making Healthy Decisions For Yourself and the Earth
    Ira Nirenberg

    1. Mathematics I. Title
    10 9 8 7 6 5 4 3 2 1 1997

ISBN 1-57706-676-6

Pi Press, A Subsidiary of Burlington National Inc.
New Orlean, LA 70118

All rights reserved, which includes the rights to reproduce this book or portions of this book. Note: Certified Teachers or University Instructors may photocopy graphs and tables, but no other text without the written permission of Pi Press.

Printed on recycled paper with water-based ink.

The text of this book was composed in Adobe Garamond.
Composition by HBIS Marketing Enterprises, Box 4762, Clifton, NJ 07015.

Cover design: Ira Nirenberg and Diana Thornton.

Printed in the USA by

Morris
PUBLISHING

3212 E. Hwy 30
Kearney, NE 68847
800-650-7888

Table of Contents

Acknowledgements

Many people have been immensely helpful to me in completing this book. First and foremost I would like to thank John Rubino (publisher of *Vegetarian Traveler Magazine*), who was the first person to read the entire manuscript. His suggestions on structure, format and clarity were invaluable. He always had an encouraging word and a great big smile—two things every writer needs. A big heartfelt thanks to Steve Kellogg, who helped to convert this book from its original Cannon software format to the Mac environment. Frank Magnuson, a colleague and friend, and his wife Sand both read the edited manuscript and helped to fine tune the book and eliminate sources of confusion. Dot Doyle, of the *North Carolina School of Science and Math*, took time out during the middle of the school year to carefully read through much of the mathematics and convinced me to change the title of Chapter 7. Dana Dell Dorson (Vice-President of *Legislation in Support of Animals—LISA*) read the manuscript and offered sound suggestions and encouraging words. Marsha Knadle, a former colleague and valued friend, spent part of her vacation reading the manuscript and offered valuable insights. A big *thank you* to my dear friend Izzy Buckweitz for reading the manuscript and offering a layperson's point of view. I would also like to thank Alan Fensin for his time and many helpful hints. Additionally, the 102 people who were kind enough to take my survey (see Appendix B), helped greatly to determine the direction and focus of my writing. This work, however, would never have existed had it not been for the *New Orleans School System* which graciously consented to give me a year long sabbatical.

I am also indebted to my sister Eileen Schram who read the manuscript, and read the manuscript, and read the manuscript…, and never once begrudgingly. She was instrumental in catching many a blooper and offering helpful suggestions. My sister is the eternal optimist and never doubted this work would be completed, which is more than I can say for myself! She is a wonderful sister and a great friend. A mega thank you to Ira Shore, who over a period of a year, taught a true tyro the basics of book publishing. He is responsible for typesetting the manuscript and getting it into camera ready form. I cannot thank him enough. More than anyone though, I thank my wife, Brenda, for reading the manuscript more times than any human being should be asked to read anything. Without her painstaking grammatical editing, her unwavering support, and her immeasurable patience, I could not have written this book. She has been a constant source of support and an intellectually challenging partner, who never let me get away with a vague sentence or an ill placed adjective. And lastly, our cat Fernie, whose passion for computer keyboards was a clear barometer for my tenacity and patience.

Clearly, many people have contributed technical and moral support. But it is the author who must take responsibility for any shortcomings this work may have.

Dedication

This book is dedicated to my mother, Sylvia Miller Nirenberg and my father, Harry M. Nirenberg. They are eternal proof that there are no substitutes for kind and loving parents.

Introduction

This is a book for the curious and the fearful, for those who would like to understand newspaper and magazine articles and "popular" books involving a modicum of mathematics. It is for anyone who remembers junior high or high school mathematics with alternating feelings of dread and boredom. Readers who had mathematics in college to fulfill a requirement, rather than a personal desire, will find the book instructive as well. Teachers and students will also find the book helpful.

The first three chapters of the book are qualitative. Chapters one and two concentrate on the failure of our educational system to create mathematically literate citizens. There is some additional commentary on problems within our society that are peripheral to mathematics education but relevant nonetheless. Chapter three, "*A Brief History of Mathematics*," is intended to put mathematics and mathematical literacy (numeracy) within the context of human development.

Chapters four, five, and six explore real-world problems. With some modest reminders, the reader is expected to operate at a seventh-grade arithmetic level.

Chapters seven and eight require no more than basic ninth-grade algebra skills which are explained within the body of the text. Again, the writing centers around real-world problems. So much so, that even if the mathematics is not fully understood after the first reading, the reader will still appreciate the problems being investigated.

Overall, the book will help people see how the need for mathematics evolved historically. It also clarifies many of the relevant parts of the subject that are essential in today's world. The emphasis is not on stating rules and giving trite examples (Sally has x coins in her pocket..., Mary is two years older than Bill..., etc.), which are the standard fare of school mathematics.

For the purpose of keeping the reader awake, no attempt is made to follow the traditional mathematics syllabus. Rather, the approach is to take timely topics and then ask the question, "What background is required to understand this problem?" For example, in chapter six, problems involving diet, inflation, and taxation are addressed by setting the scene with preliminary information that brings these problems into a more meaningful light. Problems are viewed as holistically as possible, allowing for the mathematics to evolve naturally.

Real problems have a way of reaching into many different fields. Ignoring this fact by concentrating solely on mathematics renders such problems sterile and lifeless. Mathematics, of course, has its own special value. But when applying mathematics to real-world problems, be it a simple percentage calculation or data analysis, its purpose is to aid intelligent decision making.

The style of this book is informal and nurturing, though there are no overtures regarding the topic of math anxiety. This is not to diminish the many interesting questions that the study of math anxiety raises, such as: Does math anxiety arise from poor education, or from subliminal signals that mathematics is a difficult subject that only the brightest and most gifted individuals can successfully master? Are females innately less capable in mathematics than males, or were they, at an early age, conditioned away from the subject?

Perhaps if mathematics is viewed no differently than any other subject, old psychological barriers can be overcome. To do so, context and critical thinking should be emphasized before more esoteric principles are tackled and endless drill problems assigned. After all, humanity did not begin the study of mathematics for its abstract beauty or its ability to solve meaningless problems. Conversely, it grew out of our social and economic needs.

No one book can solve all the problems created by years of frustration in the classroom. May this book be one of many in the reader's arsenal against math illiteracy.

The Problem

No subject of human concern can exist in isolation without becoming a hopeless wasteland of rules and facts. If history is a medium for charting humanity's unfolding; if literature is driven by existential themes and the social, economic, and cultural bias of the times; if art and music are expressions of the landscape of human development; then mathematics must also be seen, interpreted, and taught with the same passion and wholeness that makes any other human activity clear and alive. Colin Wilson, who has authored many intriguing books on the human condition summed it up well when he wrote, "Boredom cripples the will. Meaning stimulates it."[1]

So much of what is given to students in mathematics is without context, history, or purpose. Much of mathematics education is analogous to memorizing thousands of foreign words with the promise of someday forming meaningful sentences. Looking honestly at how the subject is presented, it is little wonder that few students see its relevance. We have taught the subject in isolation, paying lip service to meaning by creating a context that is strained and unconvincing at best.

Students are expected to operate symbolically with algebra without a clear understanding of decimals and fractions. Even those individuals who can perform basic operations do so because they have remembered a series of steps (an algorithm) for solving the problem. The question, "Why does this algorithm work?," is rarely considered. Most people have spent so much energy keeping all the rules straight in their minds, that the rationale behind the rules is overlooked. Nor is this only symptomatic of mathematics. I have known students to complete a college physics course with an A who knew no more than how to plug numbers into formulas. Others who managed B's and C's were still remarkably medieval in their view of physical reality. It is just as common for students without an understanding of basic algebra to successfully complete their requirements in calculus. They learned long ago that memorizing procedures and jumping through the appropriate "hoops" would yield passing grades. This is not to say that memorizing certain information and knowing some rules are contrary to good education. But the prevalent mechanical and rule-based approach throughout most of elementary and secondary school is devoid of comprehension and wonder, and instead, filled with fear and anxiety.

This reminds me of the science fiction classic, *"The Day the Earth Stood Still."* In the movie, Michael Rennie (the benign, though powerful alien) gives Patricia Neal (the above average human) three alien words to memorize while they are being pursued. Rennie makes it clear to Neal that if anything happens to him his bodyguard robot will wipe out our violent, primitive species. He's killed moments later, and mankind will be safe only if Neal is successful in reaching the robot and uttering the three words. Now I've seen this film several times (it is, after all, a classic) and for the life of me, and the planet, I can never remember the three alien words. Each time my memory fails, I am struck by the same thought. I picture myself in front of Rennie's robot mumbling incoherently, trying desperately to regurgitate the proper sequence of sounds. The robot (and this is the really pathetic part) amused by my stupidity, bypasses me, and goes on to make short work of the rest of the planet. My only consolation is being spared the embarrassment of having anyone know the fatal role I played.

So much of the rule-based approach and lack of context in mathematics is paralleled in this story. There is the great fear of incorrectly solving the problem and looking foolish. Students do not want anyone to know how "stupid" they are. They feel totally lost and assume everyone knows more than they do. When they are shown how to solve the problem they often admit, "I don't understand what's happening." This is a

reasonable response since they are given only instructions, not explanations, which leads to feelings of fear and inadequacy. A similar situation
(though the predominate feeling here is boredom) occurs in history
classes when the subject is debased into dates and names. Few students
can see the currency in studying, "markers in time and lots of dead people." The person who conveyed this to me also insisted that studying
what happened in the past had nothing to do with the present!
Unfortunately, poor student instruction is the first step in a chain reaction that ends with ill-trained teachers. The entire process forms a closed
repetitive loop, much like "the chicken or the egg" scenario.

In preparation to teach secondary school I took several education
courses to gain certification. In one of these courses, "Reading in the
Content Area," the teacher read us a story about an elderly woman who
loved her cats so much that when they died, not being able to part with
them, she put them into a huge freezer. The professor then began
explaining various ways to incorporate the story into our curriculum.
When my turn came, he suggested I have my students count the number of dead cats. I was teaching gifted algebra at the time! What a dis-
couraging example of the kind of advice being offered to would-be
mathematics teachers.

Given the state of mathematics instruction, it is not surprising that
large numbers of people see no point to the subject. There are, however,
those rare individuals who find the subject to be immensely interesting.
Many others could also, but it must be realized that a love of learning
and a desire to see deeper cannot exist unless a person is charmed into
the effort.

This route is best taken from an inductive approach: beginning with
the specific (concrete) and working toward the general (abstract). But if
the concrete is stripped of context, and reduced to only the rules-of-the-
game, most people will forever be amazed by anyone's scholastic inter-
ests.

Sadly, it is often too easy to condition people to see only the most
superficial aspects of mathematics. And once such a mind-set is created,
it's hard to undo. It's like convincing someone that all there is to an ice-

berg is the part seen above water. The idea to look deeper or give credence to the fantastic possibility that nine-tenths of the iceberg is below the surface would seem too incredible. What's worse, those few who would espouse such a concept would be chastised and ridiculed.

Several years ago I was asked to address a group of middle school teachers. The subject of the talk revolved around computer and calculator use in the classroom. I was an advocate for the use of both of these tools at the earliest levels of education. A number of teachers felt this to be dangerous since in their minds I was abandoning learning and replacing it with key-stroke fluency. In response to this, I asked, "How many of you teach or have taught students division with fractions?" Everyone raised their hands. I went on and asked, "How many of you feel that your students would be short changed if you were to use calculators solely in teaching this manipulation?" (Texas Instruments had just come out with a calculator that handled fraction arithmetic.) Most thought it a bad idea—many because they felt the children would not really be learning the process, and a small percentage voiced concerns that their roles as teachers were being reduced. I then asked, "Who can tell me why when dividing by fractions we are instructed to invert the denominator and then multiply it by the numerator?" In other words, why does this work? No one answered me.

For some, I think the question had never crossed their minds. Their students were expected to comprehend a series of mechanical steps without reassurance that there was a logical reason beneath the superficial rule. At worst, if the calculator was used as poorly as the handwritten mechanical approach, all the students would be doing is substituting one set of rules for another.

Instead of instructing the students to invert the denominator and then multiply this inverted number by the numerator (for example, ⅗ ÷ ⅖ = ⅗ × 7/2) we would be saying: enter the top fraction, then press the divide symbol, then enter the bottom fraction, now press the equal sign. The advantage to the second set of mindless instructions is that the magic of turning the denominator upside down is done away with. Since students are not given an explanation for inverting, it only serves to reinforce their notion that mathematics is truly mysterious.

There is, however, an added advantage to using the calculator. The instructor could introduce division with fractions by having the students do several multiplication and division problems with fractions on their calculators. (See Chapter Five for an explanation of operations with fractions.) Say for example: $2/3 \div 7/5$, followed by $2/3 \times 5/7$, and $3/4 \div 2/11$, followed by $3/4 \times 11/2$. Consider these four problems as two sets, each set containing first a division problem followed by a multiplication problem. The students would record their results and be asked if they noticed any pattern. Most would quickly see that the two problems within each set have the same answer. The students would then have an opportunity to investigate the patterns in each set of problems. Many would realize that one can turn a division problem into a multiplication problem by multiplying the denominator of the bottom fraction by the numerator of the top fraction and vice versa.

The instructional advantage is in allowing students to discover the rule for themselves and setting the stage for the more meaningful question—*Why does this work?* This process can, of course, be achieved without the use of a calculator. The calculator, however, focuses attention on the evaluation process, since less time is spent with the mundane task of manipulating the numbers. This is advantageous because information that is given too slowly loses its meaning as surely as information given too rapidly is never received. We lose comprehension if information is not received within a narrow spectrum of time and space. If you try reading the next paragraph at a rate of one word every 10 seconds, the increased time will inhibit understanding; the individual words will become more pronounced than the content of the paragraph.

Similarly, when information is too spread out in space, understanding can also be compromised. There is the interesting story of pilots who noticed large drawings carved into the Peruvian landscape. The drawings are believed to be quite ancient and have stirred all manner of hypotheses, such as alien landing strips. Such imagination stems from the fact that though the markings are indiscernible at ground level, they are clearly obvious from the air. Hence, the drawings have meaning only from a context of height.

The point is to recognize the difference between information acquisition and the information itself. The manner in which ideas are structured and presented helps determine whether people will listen and learn. Unfortunately, too many people hear nothing today.

CHAPTER TWO

Those We Leave Behind

Anyone who has traveled to a foreign country and been unfamiliar with the language knows the frustration involved in communicating. All of a sudden, so many things that were taken for granted are beyond reach. Asking a waiter if the entrée is highly salted or cooked in animal fat becomes a drawn out, uncertain affair; simple directions to the neighborhood grocery or drug store become live theater; knowing phrases like *"good morning," "no thank you,"* and *"how much?"* help to create the illusion of fluency.

My first encounter with this type of "verbal illiteracy" occurred while visiting a friend in Ecuador, South America. Armed with remnants of two years of high school Spanish, I motioned and gestured my way through the country. While lost among the hills and labyrinths of Quito, I saw a movie theater with an advertisement for an English movie. I decided to escape my alien world for a couple of hours. As it turned out, the film had been dubbed into French and had Spanish subtitles; I took my chances back on the streets.

We are spared these feelings and experiences through the familiarity and insulation of our own culture. But language takes many forms, one of which is mathematics. Newspapers print percentages and fractions; recipes are cut in thirds for smaller portions; seamstresses and carpenters insert numbers in formulas that give appropriate lengths for spacing patterns correctly on dresses and on floor tiling. Health officials authoritatively tell the public what percentage of fat in their diet is optimum. Colorful graphs are shown relating such things as fat consumption with various cancers. Linear and nonlinear trends are cited ranging from mundane hourly pay rates to the horrific figures of the human population explosion.

But graphs and statistical results cited in articles are rarely elaborated upon. Newspaper and magazine writers do not remind readers how a percentage is calculated, nor do they carry out the multiplication or division which leads to the result they quote. These skills are deemed to be in everyone's possession. Using them freely is considered part of a shared literacy inherited from our educational system.

Many calculations do not involve equations with esoteric symbols reserved for the mathematician and scientist. They belong to the realm of the seventh-grader—straight forward manipulations with simple numbers that help clarify or explain the deficit, national defense spending, or health care expenditures. The purpose of mathematics is to help the general public navigate through the uncertain eddies and currents of society. But who out there is seaworthy?

*   *   *

The scene is a public school built in the early part of this century. In better days it housed the Italian, Jewish, Irish, and Polish children of immigrants. It was a symbol of social justice and social evolution, a reaffirmation of the child labor laws that made the schoolroom, not the factory, the second home for a new generation of children. Today, fifteen hundred children are crowded into this same building that was intended to accommodate only one thousand students. The roof leaks, there are no doors on the stalls of toilets, many do not work, there is no toilet paper or soap. Textbooks are in short supply and those that are available are out of date. Classes are held on stairwell landings and in cloakrooms; there are more students than desks.

The air outside is noxious and the ground is poisoned. Industrial complexes, easily within sight of the school, produce chemical waste and solid pollutants; run-off seeps into the ground and stagnates on the concrete. The companies that produce the toxins have incorporated as a separate city and pay no taxes to the city where the school is located. Though the citizens pass local laws for higher taxes to supplement education, property values are too low and welfare and unemployment too high to correct the problem. The federal government assures each district in the country minimum foundation funding. This is a sum of money that has been estimated to be sufficient to maintain each school. But no school system relies on this money as its sole support. Affluent districts can pass property tax laws with lower percentages than poor districts and still raise more money. This means the more wealthy pay proportionately less of their income for better schools and presumably a better education. Yet minimum foundation funding is considered fair because everyone gets an equal piece of the pie; but when it comes to the rest of the meal, each community is on its own.

In another inner city the school building is in the same state of disrepair, but crowding is not a problem. Truancy rates, as with all inner city schools, are high. Many of the students are truant more often than they are in school. By the seventh or eighth grade many of them will have dropped out. They will fill the jails and welfare lines, victims of a failed system and a failed home life. They will become the illiterate parents of a new generation of children who will be society's future disposables.

This grim picture is not an exaggeration. Jonathan Kozol gives a graphic portrayal of inner city schools in his book, *Savage Inequalities*. It is highly recommended reading.

Kozol cites many disheartening statistics. Drop out rates in some inner city middle schools are between 10 and 20 percent.[1] Of those who do reach high school, an average of 50 to 60 percent will drop out.[2] In particularly bad areas the drop out rate can shoot above 80 percent.[3] There is no doubt that society has left these people behind. It has employed the same mind-set with human beings as with garbage—out of sight, out of mind. But refuse returns, washed up on beaches, poisoning the air and water, and degrading the quality of our lives. Similarly, it is impossible to live in a polarized society of haves and have-nots without the inevitable outpouring of crime and injustice spilling into our lives and poisoning our souls.

Ultimately, all of society is victimized. Millions of dollars are spent every year on a penal system to correct a problem that should never have begun. It costs New York City, $60,000 a year to maintain just one inmate in its jails. It is sobering to note that nine out of ten of the male inmates are public school dropouts.[4]

A few new buildings and good teachers will not solve this problem, though they would certainly be a flare in the darkness offering hope. Mandatory Head Start programs with compulsory parental involvement and a restructuring of social welfare laws, coupled with economic and environmental justice, are crucial. Drug education, family planning, and prenatal care are essential as well. But without education, there is no solution and there is no hope.

If the past is the key to the future, society could learn much from Caliph Hakam II, who lived in Cordoba Spain over a thousand years ago. He had a library containing over 400,000 manuscripts and maintained twenty-seven public schools for impoverished students.[5] It is not surprising that the Arabs were the most powerful and affluent people at a time when Western Europe was immersed in the Dark Ages.

Few inner city citizens will be ready for the twenty-first century. In truth, a large number of our "educated" population may not fare much better than the destitute of today. A large percentage of America's jobs are shifting from manufacturing into the service and information fields. Most of the remaining jobs in the manufacturing and service sector will increasingly become automated. Present jobs in factories, retail shops, supermarkets, and the fast food industry will vanish. Even the newspaper boy may be facing extinction. When home computers become as common as telephones and data base systems become more universal and versatile, the printed word will decline. Why waste the resources to produce millions of newspapers and employ all the people to produce the physical item, when many people will subscribe to the paper by computer? When a hard copy of an article is desired it can easily be printed. As technology and computers improve, even people with skilled and white collar jobs will join the unemployed. One striking example of this will be in the field of computer technology itself. Many professionals make their living by instructing others how to use computers, in both the business and home environment. But one of the research goals for artificial intelligence is to make the computer as user friendly as possible. These young professionals who train others on computer systems, may find, in 20 or 30 years, that they will be as employable as a horse salesman would be today. Consider an example from the past.

The year is 1890 and Zeke makes a modest living by selling horses in the New York City area. Automobiles are, at best, experimental. But over the next 30 years the automobile will transform the American city. Depending on how old our friend Zeke is, he may be put out to pasture with his horses.

Our world is undergoing an incredible information and technological revolution. The good jobs of today may be nonexistent in two or three decades. To paraphrase author, teacher, and artist Paul Hewitt: In today's changing world we need to cultivate our ability to learn; learning how to learn is fundamental to our survival.[6]

Our work force is comprised of people who have not been taught problem solving skills or critical thinking in school. They were given rules and formulas, and dates and names to memorize from grade school through college. How many fertile imaginations have been abandoned to rote instruction? Mathematician and writer Tobias Dantzig realized this problem over sixty years ago when he wrote: "... our school curricula, by stripping mathematics of its cultural content and leaving a bare skeleton of technicalities, have repelled many a fine mind."[7] Both Dantzig and Caliph Hakam would be disappointed in our progress.

Numerous studies report the poor performance of high school students in the United States. Every four years a congressionally mandated program through the National Assessment of Educational Progress (NAEP), is administered to school children. The 1990

NAEP Report Card stated:

> All the high school seniors demonstrated success with third-grade material. However, [only] 91 percent showed mastery of the fifth-grade course, indicating that not all students are graduating from high school with [even] a grasp of how to apply the four basic arithmetic operations to solve simple problems with whole numbers. Fewer than half ... demonstrated a consistent grasp of decimals, percents, fractions, and simple algebra, and only 5 percent [even lower than in the 1986 NAEP] showed an understanding of geometry and algebra that suggested preparedness for the study of advanced mathematics.[8]

According to the NAEP test only 46 percent of twelfth-graders could operate at a seventh-grade level in mathematics.[9] Bear in mind that this does not represent 46 percent of all 18 year-olds, since a good many drop out before twelfth grade.

If these statistics are not startling enough, consider the fact that the top 10 percent of American students competed in an international math and science test and placed thirteenth out of a total of fifteen.[10] Taiwan and Korea were in first and second places respectively for the math test and exchanged places for the science test. America managed to beat out Jordan and Spain in math and Jordan and Ireland in science. Japan did not compete. Considering the present economic status of America compared to that of Jordan, Spain, and Ireland, it comes as no surprise that The Carnegie Commission on Science, Technology, and Government would state that our present educational status is, "a chronic and serious threat to our nation's future."[11]

There is, of course, the possibility that only the best from our top group will seek college and graduate degrees. And that our universities and colleges will act as filters assuring America of well educated teachers, scientists, doctors, and lawyers.

In an effort to see how true this might be, I conducted my own informal survey. The survey was really a test composed of 10 basic arithmetic problems. Since I was curious to see how much of the mathematical manipulations adults retain after leaving school, no cal-culators were permitted. Anyone with at least four years of college and U.S. educated could participate, except those holding degrees in math, physics, or engineering. (It seemed too ludicrous to assume this group would lack arithmetic skills.) The study was conducted at several of the coffee houses in the New Orleans area. Most of the per-sons frequenting coffee houses are college graduates, with a fair num-ber of medical doctors, lawyers, teachers, and PhDs thrown in for good measure. Another advantage is that many of these people are transplants from all over the country, thus providing for more of a national, rather than regional, sampling.

All the surveys were completed in my presence. A small number of people refused to participate. (It was interesting to note how their body language abruptly became closed and frightened when they were told the purpose of the survey.) Most, however, though assuring me of poor results, were kind enough to take the test. Some of the parameters and results of the test are as follows:

1. 57 women and 45 men participated for a total of 102 people.
2. 56 of the participants (32 women and 24 men) had completed more than four years of college.
3. Ages ranged 21-72
4. 46 could not add two fractions with unlike denominators.
5. 42 could not divide one fraction by another.
6. 40 out of 99 could not compute a "fraction of a fraction."
7. 25 could not work with simple percentages.

(*A complete description of this study, including the test and the answers, can be found in Appendix B.*)

This is frightening. Those who took part in the study are among the most educated in America. In 1987, less than 20 percent (1 in 5) Americans had completed four years or more of college.[12] If the assumption is made that those adults who completed college are more mathematically literate than those who did not, it implies that as many as 9 out of 10 adults in America cannot add two fractions with unlike denominators. (This worst case scenario is estimated by assuming that roughly one-half of all college graduates cannot do the operation—according to my study. Since only 1 out of 5 people are college graduates, half this number gives one out of ten who can perform the operation, or 9 out of 10 who cannot.) The implication is that of those twelfth-graders who can perform seventh-grade arithmetic, according to the NAEP test cited previously, few will retain such skills as adults.

It could be argued that since people do not add unlike fractions on a daily basis, they merely "lose what they do not use." To a degree this makes sense since their ability to perform the needed operations extends no further than the steps they had memorized to solve the problem—that is, no **real** learning was ever done. However, the above reason does not explain the fact that a significant number of educated people cannot compute simple percentages which are needed regularly at supermarkets and restaurants.

Many books are published today to keep the layperson informed in math and science. Some are excellent renditions of difficult subjects without the rigor that would accompany the work in a professional setting. Because of this, the author or reviewer will assume the book is easily within reach of most people. But few, if any, of these books are really suited for the typical college graduate, let alone the "average man on the street."

An excellent book written by John Allen Paulos titled *Innumeracy* has received a good deal of exposure and acclaim. Paulos informs us in the introduction that: "The approach throughout (the book) is gently mathematical, using some elementary ideas from probability and statistics which, though deep in a sense, will require nothing more than common sense and arithmetic."[13] True as this statement is, my experience has shown that unless the reader of this book has some math/science background, too many basic arithmetical skills are assumed. A large number of college educated people would find *Innumeracy* a sizable challenge. Paulos is not unaware of this fact and states, "... I'm convinced that a sizable minority of adult Americans wouldn't be able to pass a simple test on percentages, decimals, fractions, and conversions from one to another."[14] I would differ with the phrase, "sizable minority", preferring "sizable majority" for the overall adult population and "sizable minority" (at the very least) for the college educated population. This is not a trivial point. For as good as *Innumeracy* is, the majority of "innumerates" will be left behind.

Ian Stewart is a British mathematician who often writes articles and books for the general public. In his delightful book *Game, Set and Math* he writes:

> To me, mathematics is fun, ... Mind you, I can understand **why** most people find that statement baffling. To see why mathematics is fun, you have to find the right perspective. You have to stop being over-awed by symbols and jargon, and concentrate on **ideas**; you have to think of mathematics as a friend, not as an enemy. I'm not saying that mathematics is always a joyous romp; but you should be able to enjoy it, at whatever level you operate.[15]

Perhaps the British are more mathematically astute than we are. But I can't help wondering—Does Stewart realize just how remedial most American's mathematics "levels" are?

One final quote, an excerpt from the jacket cover of *Relativity* by Albert Einstein reads: "Here is a book, however, by the originator of the theory himself explaining the theory in simple words that anyone with the equivalent of a high school education can understand." Perhaps this statement is true in theory, but not in practice! All joking aside, a theory is a very substantial statement, not to be confused with opinions or hypotheses.

It is not my desire to be a detractor for any of these books. They are all excellent. The point is to recognize that what are called "popular math and science books" (which are written to help us stay current in a quickly changing world) are reserved for a small minority of our population. They will not be read by the poor illiterates who fill our inner cities, nor will they be read by the numerous college graduates we have left behind.

CHAPTER THREE

A Brief History of Mathematics

Precounting and Primitive Counting

Historically, what we have needed to know depended on where and when we lived, and who we were. Humans as hunters and gatherers needed few number skills. A sense of "larger and smaller than," an ability to pair-off two different sets of objects, and some modest counting skills, would have made a person very mathematically literate in paleolithic times (40 thousand years ago). Alternatively, the early Stone Age dweller who could not evaluate which pile of food was larger probably stood a dim chance of passing on any progeny. From a paleolithic perspective then, simple counting skills would have exhausted mathematical knowledge.

In precounting societies, an ability to form a one-to-one correspondence between different sets of objects would be immensely helpful. For example, counting is unnecessary in pairing one male to one female (assuming a monogamous society). Those left unpaired, being the same sex, might be encouraged to seek greener pastures elsewhere or to play a differentiated role within their group. Anthropological correctness aside, this pairing ability would be invaluable in a primitive communal setting—even if the task is just to distribute an equal share of berries to each member of the tribe.

No one knows exactly when the ability to pair off objects emerged for man. But evidence of bones with notches carved into them suggests that humankind has been keeping records in this manner for at least thirty or forty thousand years.[1] Many scholars believe that this mathematical innovation led eventually to written language.[2] The same idea is still practiced today, when a line is drawn each time an event occurs. It's the old cliche of the prisoner who scratches a mark on the wall each day to keep track of time. A notable version of this concept is the story of Cinderella. Remember how the prince goes from lady to lady trying to find the best fit for the glass slipper? Here there is only one acceptable pairing, yet numerous unsuccessful correspondences are required in order to finally isolate the one correct match. Cinderella belongs to the genre of stories where the hero must find a unique correspondence (for example, the matching pieces of a cryptic medallion) that will prove he is the rightful heir to the throne, or give him the power to claim any throne he wants.

The practice today of receiving a receipt for a business transaction is a sophisticated example of the above idea. When paleolithic man bartered he probably employed a similar method of keeping track of the number of items in question. Both parties could keep a bone with the same number of notches representing the trade. The same idea exists in the form of the modern tally stick, which governments, such as Great Britain, used into the early nineteenth century for tax keeping purposes.[3]

*   *   *

During the last several centuries Western man has discovered populations of indigenous people who live as their stone age ancestors did. Studying their cultures has helped to advance our understanding of the way number systems evolved.

Counting systems were no doubt long in the making. After all, the sophistication of a counting system is linked to the demands of the people who use it. The amount of numbers required in a number system is directly tied to the complexity of the society in question. It would be difficult, for example, to imagine a paleolithic people using even three digit numbers. Not because of a lack of intelligence in dealing with such numbers as one or two hundred, but because of for any practical application of them.

George Gamow, in his classic book, *One, Two, Three ... Infinity*, tells of an African tribe called the Hottentot who do not have names for numbers beyond three. The Hottentot count: one, two, three, many.[4]

In Graham Flegg's book, *Numbers: Their History and Meaning*, there is the example of another African tribe called the Damara of Namibia who cannot count beyond two. To quote Flegg: "... the Damara of Namibia, who were prepared to exchange more than once a sheep for two rolls of tobacco but would not simultaneously exchange two sheep for four rolls."[5]

All counting systems display patterns, but the more primitive the system, the faster the onset of repetition. The following examples from Flegg will clarify this idea. A tribe of aborigines living near the Torres Strait between Australia and New Guinea count only up to five as reproduced below:

one: urapon   four: okosa-okosa
two: okosa   five: okosa-okosa-urapon
three: okosa-urapon

Another aboriginal counting system goes up to six as follows:

one: mal   four: bularr-bularr
two: bularr   five: bularr-guliba
three: guliba   six: guliba-guliba

The above two number systems have the patterns:

one	two-two-one	one	two-three
two		two	three-three
two-one		three	
two-two		two-two	

Counting, though seen as a simple procedure, is not. It probably took thousands of years for human beings to understand the concept of a number devoid of an object—an understanding of "twoness" as opposed to two "somethings." The various ways the number two is expressed today in English may serve as a linguistic fossil record of our own slow progress toward number abstraction.

Consider some of the synonyms for the number two: pair, couple, twain, brace, yoke, deuce, couplet, set, team, and twin. On the other hand, we do not have a multitude of synonyms for numbers like 253. Larger numbers probably came into use after we had abstracted counting; when we no longer needed the concrete crutch of associating a number with a particular set of things. It is revealing to find a word like thrice in our own language with the double meaning of three and greatly. A throw-back to when we counted one, two, many? In fact, in the Indo-European counting systems, the "early words for three can be linked to a root word whose meaning was beyond."[6]

Everyone realizes there is no limit to counting. Our present day number system can accommodate any number large or small. But how well do people use and understand large and small (microscopically small) numbers today? Anyone who doesn't know there are two tens in twenty is handicapped in our society. What about the person who doesn't know how many millions there are in a billion, or a trillion? It is plausible that many educated people today count: 1,2,3...1,000,000, many. Is it possible that these individuals are as limited within our own society as an aborigine is within his own culture, who can't count beyond two? How then, has the need for numeracy changed throughout history, and how much do people really need to know today?

Number Systems

There is a formidable gap in our understanding of the evolution of mathematics. At best, we can make some educated guesses about pre-counting societies and primitive counting systems. But thousands of years stand between these skills and a developed number system employing arithmetical principles. By the fourth to fifth millennium B.C. there is clear evidence that mathematics of a highly abstract nature already existed. The oldest known mathematical document was written by an Egyptian named Ahmes around 1700 B.C.. It is commonly referred to as the Ahmes or Rhind Papyrus. (Rhind was a Scottish antiquarian who purchased the papyrus in 1858.) We know from Ahmes that the papyrus he wrote was based on even earlier works; possibly from as far back as five thousand years ago. Ahmes refers to his work as "... the knowledge of all existing things and all obscure secrets."[7] We see that mathematics was not thought of as belonging to the masses, since "obscure secrets" were usually reserved for the priesthood.

Ahmes had 84 problems on the papyrus.[8] Many of these problems were algebraic. Evidently, solving for an unknown quantity is a very old concept. And since Egyptian mathematics centered around practical problems, algebra must have been used as long as five thousand years ago with problems involving weighing, measuring, and land surveying and parceling. None of the problems were explained and only rote instructions were given for solutions. Thousands of years later in Europe during the Renaissance, mathematicians were still reluctant to divulge their proofs. One reason for this was that problems were often given as challenges and as a means of promotion or instatement in universities. It appears this tradition of vagueness is alive and well in many schools today. All too often, mathematics is taught as a series of steps that magically produce correct answers.

Because of the Ahmes Papyrus, scholars believed for many years that Egyptian mathematics was the oldest and most advanced. However, about one hundred years ago, archaeologists learned to read the Summerian wedge shaped writing, Cuneiform, which is the oldest writing known. (If not for the discovery of the Rosetta Stone in 1799, Egyptian Hieroglyphics would have remained as much a mystery as Summerian Cuneiform.) A knowledge of Cuneiform led scholars to conclude that the Babylonians were more adept at mathematics than the Egyptians. It is now believed that the Babylonians developed the first place-value system in the world.

The place-value system is taught in the early elementary grades; remember learning about the ones, tens, hundreds, thousands, ...

columns? Well it took thousands of years before some clever
Babylonian thought up the novel idea of using position to describe
amount. Here was a way to use a small number of symbols to represent any quantity. Take, for example, the numerals 1 and 9. Ordering
the numerals as 1 followed by 9 gives nineteen; in reverse, it is nine-
ty-one. In our present system we use 10 symbols (0-9) and depending upon how we place them we can write any number. Contrast this
to Egyptian numerals, where position played no role. The number 12
would have been understood whether written: ∩|| or ||∩
    (*See Figure 3.1 below for a list of Egyptian numerals*).

Egyptian Hieroglyphic Numerals

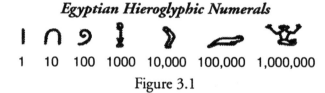

| 1 | 10 | 100 | 1000 | 10,000 | 100,000 | 1,000,000 |

Figure 3.1

The Roman number system is a bit more sophisticated than the
Egyptian, though not as useful as the earlier Babylonian system. With
Roman numbers, proper positioning serves as an abbreviation or
short-cut by using a subtraction principle. For example: IV = (5-1)
instead of IIII, IX = 10 - 1 instead of VIIII and in general, whenever
a larger number is preceded by a smaller number it is understood to
mean larger minus smaller, as in other cases like, XL = 50 - 10 and
CM = 1000 - 100. Examples of several other number systems are
given in Figure 3.2 below.

The number 23 expressed in ancient numerals.
.. ||| (Cretan)
Δ Δ ||| (Greek Attic)
× × ||| (Roman)
✧ ✧ ||| (Aztec)

Figure 3.2

A lack of concise notation, a place-value system, and an understanding of the zero concept, impeded the mathematical progress of ancient cultures. Imagine multiplying or dividing with Roman numbers. Though there are ways to do so, they are long and involved.[9] Simple calculations today required the talents of expert "mathematicians" during antiquity.

The most used number system in the world today is the decimal system which is based on the number ten, as opposed to the duodecimal system that has twelve as a base. The Babylonians, however, used a system based on 60 rather than 10, called the sexagesimal system. Therefore, instead of having a one's column ranging from 0-9 theirs was 0-59. The second column was the 60's, the third column, 60 × 60, (3600's column), the fourth column 60 × 60 × 60, and so on.

The Babylonian sexagesimal system is still in use today. Circles are divided into 360 degrees (6 × 60), and the hour and minute are multiples of sixty. Sixty is a very convenient number; it can easily be divided by: 2,3,4,5,6,10,12,15,20, and 30. Ten has only 2 and 5 as divisors, thus making 60 a simpler attractive base for purposes of division.

A little imagination helps to see how decimal systems and finally place-value systems originated. Before the development of fully operational counting systems, people may have begun to finger count to ten by pairing one object to each finger.

For numbers larger than ten, transactions could be carried out by counting sets of ten. One can imagine a farmer trading 7 sets of ten bushels of wheat for 5 sets of ten bushels of barley, or a shepherd describing the size of his flock as 3 sets of ten. We have remnants of this type of counting in our language today: The "score," for example, which represents 20, is most remembered in Lincoln's Gettysburg Address that begins, "Four score and seven years ago ... ", i.e., 87 years ago.

It was in fact quite common to keep track of the numbers of tens, hundreds, thousands, and greater multiples of ten, by placing a pebble aside for each set of ten, hundred, thousand, etc.. You can begin to see how place-value systems could develop from this—a column for counting to ten, a column for pebbles that represented the number of tens, a different set of pebbles (larger ones) after ten sets of ten were reached and so on. In fact, one of the oldest calculating machines, the abacus, is based on the principle of separating numbers into ones, tens, hundreds, etc..

Our present number system is very abstract. Yet most people see it

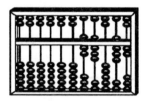

Figure 3.3 - An Abacus

as the concrete part of mathematics education today. "I can deal with numbers, but when he starts putting x's and y's on the board, forget it!," is a common retort of many students. But the only reason people deal successfully with the number system is because they are psychologically acclimated to the symbols and their meanings. Most people do not actually understand number systems. If they did, they would be able to tell you that in base 2, the number 1110 is the same as 14 in base 10. Nor would there be any opposition to converting from the present duodecimal system, used for weights and measures, to the metric system—which is decimal! (See Appendix A. page 179 for a discussion of different bases.)

In general, numbers are more difficult for us to deal with than pictures. Euclid formulated the axiomatic basis for plane geometry (picture based) in 300 B.C., while the proper group of axioms for our algebraic system (number based) was not deduced until this century.

Zeroing in on Zero

Another leap made by the Babylonians was in recognizing the need for zero. It wasn't until about the third century B.C. that they introduced the symbol (⋜) for zero.[10] Before this, the best they managed was a blank space, which is a precarious representation of zero. It makes for notational headaches and grand scale ambiguity. How can numbers like 64,000 or 6,040 or 604 be written with clarity? The Babylonians resorted to writing 604 as 6 4 (with their own numerals of course). There is little room for sloppiness here. Even after the Babylonians devised a symbol for zero, they used it only between numbers,[11] never at the end of numbers and never in calculations.[12] It was as if they were willing to concede that zero was a necessary component for a place-value system, but they still wanted as little to do with the concept as possible.

Even the Greeks who started us on the road to mathematical rigor, never dealt with it successfully. It wasn't until the Hindus developed their version of the zero concept, somewhere between 1000 and 1300 years ago, that the modern usage and symbol for zero were adopted. The intriguing question is why ancient cultures had such difficulty with the concept of "nothingness." In all likelihood, it was their inability to reconcile the notion of "nothingness" as something concrete. How, for example, could one justify the value of 10, by using the number 1 and a symbol with no value, 0?

Another more mysterious problem arises with division and zero. Division by zero is said to be undefined, yet division into zero (by 1 for example) results in zero. If zero was to be considered as merely another number, why the restriction concerning division? This must have troubled the ancients almost as much as it does present day students, when they are first confronted with the rule "thou shalt not divide by zero."

A little thought reveals why dividing by zero causes problems. There are an infinite number of points between the numbers zero and 1. The number ½ is twice as close to zero as 1 is. The number ¹⁄₁₀ is ten times closer to zero than 1. The closer we get to zero, the smaller the numbers become. Instead of dividing 1 by zero, what values would result if we divided 1 by numbers that were a hair's breadth away from zero? One divided by ½ is 2, one divided by ¹⁄₁₀ is

10, one divided by one-millionth is one million. The closer we approach zero as a divisor, the larger our answer becomes. The pattern is clear, as our divisor approaches zero, the answer continues to become larger. In the ultimate case of division by zero, we would have to say the answer is infinite and therefore undefined. (It should be understood that the above argument holds when smaller and smaller quantities are divided into numbers other than zero or infinity).

A similar argument shows that 1 divided into zero equals zero. If we divide 1 into 1, the answer is 1, but if we divide 1 into ½, one-half results. Continuing on (one divided into one-millionth, is one-millionth) we see as the dividend approaches zero so does the answer.

Confusion with Fractions—An Ancient Dilemma

Another difficult subject for the ancients was fractions. In fact, they avoided them as much as possible.[13] Fractions are strange; they have a way of changing their context without the mind realizing what has happened.

An employer with ten workers may have a payroll of five thousand dollars a week. A worker who receives five hundred dollars for the week does not regard his earnings as a fraction of five thousand dollars, but as a whole unit. A piece of pie is a fraction of a pie, but to the eater it's a **whole** piece. A person might eat a large piece of pie followed by a small piece. Two pieces were eaten, but how much of the pie was consumed? Understanding how to divide a thing into an odd number of pieces or adding two different size pieces is conceptually difficult.

Adding or subtracting fractions with different denominators means working with different pieces. The only way to work with them is to employ the concept of conversion, just as in adding feet and inches. Finding the "least common denominator" is a conversion process with each piece redefined into smaller units. In order to add one-third and one-fifth, the proper "conversion" is to cut the one-third into five equal pieces and the one-fifth into three equal pieces. Doing so, one finds that all the little pieces are now the same size and it would take fifteen of them to make a whole. There are, however, only eight pieces available so the total is eight-fifteenths. This process is the visual counterpart of finding the least common denominator (which for this case is fifteen).

Without a well-developed mathematical notational system, the kind of fraction arithmetic discussed above becomes very complicated. As previously stated, the ancients did all they could to avoid fractions, including creating finer (smaller) units of measurements so that a fraction could be restated as a new "whole" smaller unit.

The Egyptians did all their fraction arithmetic by re-expressing fractions as sums of unit fractions (fractions that have one in the numerator). For example, $5/7$ was re-expressed as, $\frac{1}{2} + \frac{1}{7} + \frac{1}{14}$, before attempting any work with the number. There was little conformity among ancient people in working with fractions. Cajori tells us: "In manipulating fractions the Babylonians kept the denominators (sixty) constant. The Romans likewise kept them constant, but equal to 12. The Egyptians and Greeks, on the other hand, kept the numerators constant, and dealt with variable denominators."[14]

Regardless of the difficulties the ancients had in working with fractions, they needed them. Therefore, societies at least four millennia ago used many of the skills taught today in seventh-grade. Though most people during this time were illiterate, the upper crust of society—the priests, engineers, scribes, bureaucrats, and skilled technician—all required mathematical knowledge. Just as today, the level of mathematics training in ancient societies depended on the individual. The level of universal literacy and numeracy that exists today (or is attempted) does so out of need, not altruism.

Money and Numeracy

Trade existed for thousands of years without the need for money. As far back as 5000 years ago, the Chinese emperor Shen Nung, set up what was probably the first "retail" market in the world.[15] No money exchanged hands, all transactions were bartered.

The natives of the Pacific island of Uap, well into the twentieth century, used "money" called fei, made of huge stone disks with holes bored out of their centers. Some of this "money" was so heavy it took at least two grown men to carry one "coin." Almost anything you can think of has been used for "money": sea shells (wampum), tobacco, animals, slaves, coconuts, tools, grains, salt, and silk were all used as a means of exchange.

Ancient societies before Greece were moneyless societies. Even though large scale trading existed between ancient countries, not a coin was ever exchanged. The Egyptians traded with the Phœnicians for wood by the boat load, and had generations of lumberjacks hacking away at the cedars of Lebanon.[16] But the wood never went through the hands of a middle man or out onto the open market; it was for the temples the Pharaohs built to honor their gods and themselves and to maintain the royal navy. Everything was run by the state. Each person had his or her particular task to perform for which they were assured a place to sleep and food to eat. The idea of "getting ahead" in the ancient world (with one exception), or in later years feudal Europe, did not exist.

Mesopotamia (ancient Babylon) may have offered the only promise for a better lifestyle in the ancient world, as described below by Charles Van Doren.

> Perhaps no other civilization besides our own has been so dependent on literacy, even though probably only one percent or fewer of Mesopotamians were ever literate, even in the best of times. Scribes, who wrote letters and kept records and accounts for kings and commoners alike, always possessed great power. As ancient advertisements for pupils and apprentices proclaimed, scribes wrote while the rest of the people worked[17]

Moneyless lifestyles have been common throughout history. The English manor, the French seigneurie, and the German

Gutsherrschaft, are all examples of self sufficient entities that existed without benefit of money.[18] The colonial period in America and frontier life were in many respects similar to such institutions.

Money, as we know it, was invented by the Greeks around the eighth century B.C.. This surprises people because it is difficult to picture a system of taxation, which the Egyptians and other ancient civilizations used, without money. But taxes were paid with grain or by a certain weight of silver or gold, but not currency as it is defined today. Buying, selling, and taxation in the contemporary sense did not exist.

The Bible can be a source of confusion concerning money concepts. In the seventeenth chapter of Genesis, God commands Abraham to circumcise any male who is eight days old, whether born in his house or "bought with money of any stranger." But according to Norman Angell in his book, *The Story of Money*, "The word here translated 'money' is in the original keseph; in the Septuagint it is correctly rendered by apyupiov, and in the Vulgate argentum; in fact, it should have been translated 'silver,' not 'money.'"[19]

When the Greeks introduced coinage in the late eighth century B.C., they laid the foundation for our modern world. Money is freedom. Without money, a fair exchange is difficult and time consuming. Only in static societies where commodities never change, in kind or quantity, can simple barter systems work efficiently. Otherwise, you may be trading a cow for 100 pair of shoes just to get your cow's worth. With money came opportunities unthought of in moneyless societies. Money made societies more dynamic and complex. The necessity to understand a denominational system—computing costs, making change, and paying taxes—required more computing skills for a larger part of humanity. All free men were now obliged to learn money concepts in order to function in their world. It became more important for people to use fractions in daily affairs. Being able to make change and understand new taxes became part of the new literacy and numeracy. Even those who looted and killed needed to become money literate.

During the sixth century B.C., Athens experienced the first money crisis in history. Too much easy credit caused too many commercial ventures which failed (sound familiar?). This put the borrowers in debt and left the lenders empty-handed. The importation of cheap grain from places like Italy by Greek merchants caused Athenian grain to be less valued, which in turn only caused more people to go belly-up. The situation was worsened when small farmers used their wives, children, and themselves for collateral (human chattel). Lenders, who took possession, had to feed and cloth their property, but since Athenian agriculture was in a slump, and slaves were abundant, the lenders were better off not collecting. This was a monetary disaster that threatened the fabric of Athenian culture.

Though the Greeks suffered other money crises, they did manage to patch things up for a while. Solon, a popular Athenian, is credited with implementing an innovative and successful economic plan. As part of his plan he outlawed human chattel and devalued the currency by 27 percent.[20]

Any time money is devalued it hurts those who lend, since the money they are paid back with is worth less than the money they loaned. As an exaggerated example of devaluation, let's say each dollar is devalued so that it is worth only ten cents. This means each dollar has lost 90 percent of its value or has been devalued 90 percent. Since the value of the merchandise hasn't changed, more money will be needed to purchase the same goods. Since each "dollar" is now worth only ten cents, ten "dollars" is needed to purchase what before cost one dollar.

This was the only instance in Athenian history that such an intentional devaluation occurred.[21] Solon's economic reform package involved much more than outlawing chattel and currency debasement, but we needn't go further into it for our purposes. Suffice it to say, though many were displeased, his reforms were successful. And if you're putting yourself in the position of the lender, remember, Solon only devalued the currency by 27 percent. Which means 100 pennies would have the buying power of 73 pennies (100 − 27 = 73) or roughly, it would take about four dollars to buy what had cost three dollars previously. This can be seen by rounding 27 percent to 25 percent for ease of calculation. With each dollar worth 25 percent less (or 75 cents), 4 new "dollars" equals three old dollars. Clearly, this type of monetary manipulation causes a lack of faith in the currency of a nation. It also goes to show why printing too much money causes inflation; the more dollars in circulation the less they are worth and so your money buys less and less. From a practical point of view, inflation and devaluation are the same thing. (Inflation will be discussed more in chapter six.)

The Golden Age of Greece and Mathematical Thought

The period 600-300 B.C. is considered the Golden Age of Greece. Not surprisingly, Greek mathematics began to flourish at this time. Pythagoras (who may never have existed) is credited with forming a group called the Pythagoreans who were possibly the first to do mathematical research.[22] Most of Greek mathematics and science was based on geometry and arithmetic with whole numbers. (Fractions were used, but the Greeks considered them only as ratios of whole numbers.) Greek mathematics during the early part of the Golden Age was inseparable from metaphysics. When it was discovered that certain numbers were not expressible as simple fractions, a mathematical, as well as a metaphysical, crisis arose.

Consider a right triangle whose legs (base and height) measure one inch. (Figure 7.6 in Chapter 7 page 135 can be considered a generic right triangle.) The hypotenuse (the line connecting the two legs) will have a length of the square root of two inches. The square root of two cannot be represented as a ratio of whole numbers and is therefore defined as an **irrational** number. Furthermore, any attempt to find the exact value of the square root of two yields an unending, nonrepetitive sequence of numbers. Using a calculator to find the square root of two, fills the screen with numbers beginning 1.41— only the display area of the calculator prevents the numbers from continuing on forever. This was a metaphysical nightmare for people who believed geometry and whole numbers were expressions of perfection. A finite length, easily seen and easily constructed, represented by an unending number? A length not expressible as a ratio of two whole numbers? Such concepts violated the basic premise upon which Greek intellectual and metaphysical thought were based.

The ancient Greeks believed the universe was harmoniously governed by "perfect" geometric structures (circles and spheres, for example) and simple arithmetical ratios. Heaven was perfection, (for Plato), and the Earth was a coarse, shadowy, representation of that perfection.

It could be argued that we still have a preferential way of viewing reality. In principle, we agree with the ancient Greeks regarding perfection and symmetry in nature, though we no longer differentiate between heaven and Earth. The notion that the universe is explainable in terms of the language of mathematics, is at the heart of all physical science today.

Though not bound to the few "perfect" geometric figures of the Pythagoreans, the search today is for mathematical symmetry. Modern physics relies on the "symmetry" of physical laws. Physicists speak of "beautiful" theories, where beauty often refers to mathematical equations that easily describe these symmetries. The brilliant physicist, Paul Dirac, once said he preferred beauty to accuracy in describing reality. One wonders whether we have been subliminally conditioned to search for beauty in nature because of Greek tradition, or if it is an innate part of the human psyche to do so.

By 300 B.C., Euclid (the man responsible for your studying tenth grade geometry) had organized the subject into 10 axioms from which he deduced all geometrical "truths." The organization and methodology that Euclid brought to human thought was analogously as unifying, and evolutionary, as any political reconfiguration the world has ever known.

Though Greece passed on, its accomplishments remained. It enriched the empire of Alexander the Great, maintained Byzantium while Western Europe fell into darkness, and found a home (via the Hindus) in the Muslim world. It provided for Europe's Renaissance and even today continues to be a source of insight for classical and modern thinkers. Even Rome, an intellectual lightweight at best, saw the value in learning from the Greeks—when she wasn't destroying them.

Numeracy, the Dark Ages, and the Crusades

By 1 A.D., Rome had absorbed Greece and had incorporated many of its economic ideas into her own system. She boasted a middle and merchant class and money was a common financial device. Of course, most Roman citizens were still innumerate. But those who lived in Rome proper found books easy to come by and were fluent in the arithmetic of money.[23]

Gold coins were used for imperial payments, and taxes were payable in gold, silver, and copper coinage; ordinary transactions of every day life were carried out in small denominational copper coins.[24] The same basic money skills we find necessary today were equally important 2000 years ago.

The responsibilities of the educated classes in democratic Greece and republican Rome were similar in many respects to our own. Electing politicians who understood the role of trade and its affect on currency, the need for stability in the market place, and an internally consistent point of view, were just as important then as now. However, when the Western Roman Empire fell in the fifth century A.D., literacy took a nose dive in Roman-controlled Germany, France, England, the Netherlands, Belgium, Switzerland, and Italy. (It is convenient to cite the names of these countries even though none of them existed in their present form at this time.) Western Europe plunged into the Dark Ages, where no middle or merchant class would exist again for over six hundred years. The need therefore for basic arithmetical skills, dwindled with the loss of commerce, coins, and culture. England in 1000 A.D. had less educated people than

Rome in 1 A.D.. Western Europe was so backward in 1000 A.D. that even many monks were illiterate. Ironically, Bibles and Greek classics were at times copied by monks who mimicked the script without the slightest idea of what they were writing.[25] (Almost the kind of "work" done in many mathematics classes today.)

Dirk J. Struik puts the level of Western European mathematics during the Middle Ages in perspective, when he writes: "During the early centuries of Western feudalism we find little appreciation of mathematics even in the monasteries. In the again primitive agricultural society of this period the factors stimulating mathematics, even a directly practical kind, were nearly nonexistent ..."[26]

Though mathematics stagnated for hundreds of years in Western Europe, both the Byzantine (Eastern Roman Empire) and the Muslim Empires used and advanced the subject. The Byzantine Empire which extended as far west as Sicily was a catalyst for the revival of trade, commerce, and mathematics in what was once the southern part of the Western Roman Empire. As a result of this, the Italian cities of Genoa, Venice, and Pisa were trading with the Far East by the eleventh and twelfth centuries. In fact, trade, commerce, and competition had accelerated so much during this period, that by the early thirteenth century, Venetian merchants convinced the leaders of the Fourth Crusade to attack Constantinople (the capital of the Byzantine Empire). With Constantinople in Western hands, the Venetian merchants had a more exclusive trading arrangement with the Far East. Though the intent of the Crusades was to liberate Jerusalem from the Seljuk Turks, they played the more important role of exposing backward Europeans to culture and education. They also helped to solidify the West's interest in the Far East, which as we will see later, indirectly led to a renewed interest in navigation and mathematics.

After the Crusades began their revitalizing process, it became imperative for the West to maintain accessible and safe trade routes to the East. But when Constantinople fell to the Ottoman Turks in 1453, Europe lost her route to the East. Many historians place the beginning of the modern age at this date since it initiated a more extensive search for alternative routes east which led to the Age of Discovery.

*   *   *

There is no simple way to encapsulate the last five hundred years of human history. The changes which have occurred from the late fifteenth century to the present are monumental. If we take a long view of human history, the last 15,000 years for example, we would see humanity modestly moving along an essentially straight-line path except for three events that have significantly altered its course and speed: the Agricultural Revolution, the Age of Discovery—punctuated by the permanent migrations of Europeans across the Atlantic, and the Industrial Revolution.

Our understanding of the events that led up to the Agricultural Revolution is at best speculative. The Age of Discovery and the Industrial Revolution, in contrast, have been etched quite well onto paper and into our minds, thanks to the inventions of writing and complex language.

Modern history is full of examples highlighting the increasing need for numeracy within society. We will therefore conclude chapter three with some historical examples and their relationship to numeracy.

Numeracy and the New World

Fourteen hundred ninety-two is a popular date because it ushered in the age of European exploration and exploitation. As every school child is taught, Columbus believed he had reached the Indies, hence we have "Indians" in North America. Believing he had reached the Indies, however, is at the bottom of Columbus's list of errors. Before going any further, let us dispel the myth that Columbus proved the world was round. This was the furthest thing from his mind. Ancient Greek knowledge that the world was round had reached the West, so

any educated European knew this. The real question during the
fifteenth century was not the shape of the world, but its size and
geography.
Columbus appears to have favored arguments that supported a
smaller circumference for the earth and a larger land mass for Asia.
This made travel to the East using a western sea route seem more fea-
sible.
Columbus spent ten years trying to convince European monarchs
that by sailing west, he could reach the East Indies. Most monarchs,
however, had advisors who discouraged the enterprise. Few advisors
accepted Columbus's notions regarding the size of the Earth and the
extent of Asia.
The bottom line is that Columbus was lucky. To quote Timothy
Ferris:

> Columbus's plan appeared foolhardy to anyone who possessed a realis-
> tic sense of the dimensions of the earth. To sail westward to Asia, as
> the geographers of the court at Castile took pains to inform
> Columbus, would require a voyage lasting approximately three years,
> by which time he and his men would surely be dead from starvation or
> scurvy.[27]

Much of what Columbus believed was based more on personal
bias than existing knowledge. For example, he put much stock in a
reference from the Apocryphal Book of the Old Testament, Esdras(II
Esd. 6:42) which says, "Six parts hast thou dried up."[28] From this he
inferred sixth-sevenths of the world was dry land.
Believing that he had reached the Indies, Columbus said, "Neither
reason nor mathematics nor maps were any use to me."[29] Ironically,
he was correct, since no amount of mathematics could predict, and
no known map contained, the lands between Europe and Asia.
Additionally, the only reason Columbus obtained the necessary funds
to set sail was because Ferdinand and Isabella decided they had little
to loose and much to gain if Columbus was right; the king and
queen played a long shot that paid off.

Some eighteen hundred years before Columbus set sail, the Greek thinker Eratosthenes measured the circumference of the Earth and came to within 4 percent of the modern value. Mathematically, only the concept of **direct proportionality** (taught in seventh-grade) is needed to perform this calculation. We will discuss Eratosthenes's method below and in Chapter 7 extend these ideas beyond this "special linear case."

Before we begin the mathematics there are two things we need to state. These are:

1. The Earth is assumed to be a perfect sphere (it is actually an oblate spheroid).
2. A circle has 360°.

If you travel from the north pole to the equator this represents ¼ of the circumference of the planet. In angular measurement this amounts to 90° (¼ of 360°). It also represents roughly 6000 miles. Since our goal is to find the entire distance around the planet, we can set up a proportion as follows:

6000 miles is to 90° as ? miles is to 360°

or in a simpler form, where all degree measurements are placed on one side and miles on the other:

360°/90° = ? miles/6000 miles

Since the left-hand side equals 4, we must ask, "What number will 6000 go into four times?" The answer is, of course, 24,000. Therefore, the Earth is roughly 24,000 miles in circumference (actually it is closer to 24,900 miles).

If you felt this problem had more steps in it than necessary, you'd be correct! Once you knew one-fourth of the circumference was 6000 miles, all you needed to do was quickly multiply by 4. Eratosthenes, however, did not travel 6000 miles; in fact, he probably did not travel at all. As it turns out, he was told that on the first day of summer in Syene (now Aswan, Egypt) the sun was directly overhead (at its zenith) and cast no shadow. He lived 500 miles due north in Alexandria, and on the same day at the same time (12:00 noon) a stick in the ground at Alexandria casts a shadow of 7.5°. In other words, the angle that Eratosthenes had was not the 90° in our simplified example, but 7.5°. Using the same process as before we have:

$$7.5° \text{ is to } 500 \text{ miles as ? miles is to } 360°$$

or again, more simply:

$$360°/7.5° = \text{? miles}/500 \text{ miles}$$

If it was as obvious to us that 7.5° represented ⅟₄₈ of a circle, as it was when 90° represented ¼ of a circle, we again could forego the process of taking a ratio and using degrees, and immediately multiply 500 by 48.

It is uncertain whether Columbus was aware of Eratosthenes result, or for that matter, if he would have cared. From what we know Columbus relied heavily on the writings of the Frenchman Pierre d'Ailly,[30] who was acquainted with the work of Ptolemy—the ancient authority on astronomical and geographical matters. As it turns out, d'Ailly disagreed with Ptolemy about the extent of Asia. d'Ailly believed it was larger than Ptolemy did, thus shortening the voyage westward. On the other hand, Ptolemy disagreed with Eratosthenes about the size of the Earth, claiming it to be smaller. Columbus, in his effort to make the voyage as easy as possible, followed d'Ailly concerning the extent of Asia, and followed Ptolemy concerning the circumference of the Earth. Columbus's reasons were hardly scientific. Basically, they were a mixture of wishful thinking and religious dogma. Ironically, it was Eratosthenes's approach that guided Ptolemy and the geographers of the Renaissance, including Columbus. The problem was one of miscalculating the initial distance between two north-south points, which led to an incorrect proportion between surface distance and angular distance. Ptolemy and several prominent Renaissance geographers were led to calculate a smaller globe due to erroneous information. Columbus's error was in favoring such calculations.

It is only fair, however, to give Columbus his due. Though fortune was with him by obstructing his voyage with two large continents, travel in an east-west direction during this time period was perilous. A major difficulty for navigators up until the second half of the eighteenth century was in determining location along an east-west (longitude) line. North-south measurements (latitude) were easily taken by observing the change in location of a given star, or the sun, with respect to the horizon; such methods to determine latitude had been used for thousands of years. But discerning longitude is a nontrivial problem requiring a complicated mathematical process, unless a precise time piece is available. Since no seaworthy clock of this precision existed until 1761, navigators had to be mathematically able. A quote from Daniel Boorstin highlights the growing role of mathematics during this period:

> ... the problem of longitude (was) an educational as well as technological problem. The great seafaring nations optimistically organized mathematics courses for **common sailors** (my emphasis). When Charles II set up a mathematics course for forty pupils at Christ's Hospital, the famous 'Bluecoat' charity school in London, teachers found it hard to satisfy both the sailors and the mathematicians. The governors of the school, noting that Drake, Hawkins, and other great sailors had done well enough without mathematics, asked whether future sailors really needed it. On the side of mathematics, Sir Isaac Newton argued that the old rule of thumb was no longer good enough. 'The Mathematicall children, being the flower of the Hospitall, are capable of much better learning, and when well instructed and bound out to skilful Masters may in time furnish the Nation with a more skilful sort of Sailors, builders of Ships, Architects, Engineers, and Mathematicall Artists of all sorts, both by Sea and Land, than France can at present boast of.' Samuel Pepys, then Secretary to the Admiralty, had already set up a naval lieutenant's examination which included navigation and, following Newton's advice, naval schoolmasters were actually put on board ships to instruct the crew in mathematics.[31]

I have gone to the trouble to extensively quote Boorstin because we see a similar attitude, voiced by the "governors of the school," regarding the value of mathematics that many people still hold today—namely, "What do we need it for?" Newton's quote also gives us a sense of how relevant mathematics was becoming to the average British citizen from a political vantage point, as well as the upward mobility that an education in applied mathematics could afford a "common" person.

There is an interesting parallel here between the literacy we associate with the written word and mathematics. No scribe in ancient times worried about going hungry. The ability to read and write assured an individual a comfortable lifestyle, free of manual labor; few people had such fortune. But something very interesting has occurred since the Industrial Revolution of the mid-eighteenth century. Reading and writing became necessities for everyone. During the early years of the twentieth century, universal literacy permitted a person to stay monetarily afloat (usually), avoiding many turbulent economic storms. However, since 1950, the basic skills of universal literacy no longer assure one of a better life. What has become more apparent during the second half of the twentieth century is the ever increasing value of a good math and science background. After all, the person working on an assembly line in 1950 was probably as well educated, if not more so, than those ancient scribes who lived better than most people 3000 to 4000 years ago. But today, the equivalent of an ancient scribe is one who is well versed in mathematics and science, in that such skills set him apart from the rest of society and hold so many additional life options and opportunities.

Seamen back in the eighteenth century put algebra, geometry, and trigonometry to use in the practical world of navigation. Still, it would have been preferable to have an efficient time keeping device to eliminate complicated mathematical calculations. As we all know, the more intricate a mathematical process (or any process) the more room there is for error. A slight miscalculation in longitude could mean anything from a delayed ship to one that ran aground. Delays could have serious economic and military consequences wherein companies could lose large profits and naval commanders might lose the battle, if not the war.

The importance of longitude cannot be overstated. Its relationship to practical mathematics and astronomy, and its historical connection to commerce and war are formidable. A brief description of it follows.

Since the Earth rotates west to east, (looking down from the north pole, the Earth would appear to turn counter-clockwise) it is possible to determine your position if you know the time difference between your present location and some reference point. Since it takes the sun 24 hours to apparently complete one revolution around the Earth (meaning it appears at the same point in the sky in 24 hours) the sun must be traversing 15° each hour: 360°/24 hours = 15°/hour. Therefore, we can relate one hour to fifteen degrees. For example, when it is noon in Cape May, New Jersey, it will be exactly 9:00 A.M. in Santa Barbara, California, and Heppner, Oregon and Ephrata, Washington, since all of these cities are 45° west of Cape May. Of course in our day-to-day world, we don't worry about being so exact. For convenience we define time zones and assign all cities within each zone the same time, even though they are not all on the same longitude line.

A British navigator of the nineteenth-century, whose clock was set to London time, had no problem determining his longitude. Regardless of what happened at sea, he needed to only note the position of the sun and its relationship to the time on his clock. If, for example, the sun was at high noon in his present location and his clock read 3:30 P.M., he was three and one-half hours or 52.5° (15°/hour × 3.5 hours) west of London. If his latitude hadn't changed since he set course, this would place him near the coast of Newfoundland.

* * *

Exploration and colonization instilled greater life into trade, commerce, and technology for Southern and Western Europe during the sixteenth, seventeenth, and eighteenth centuries. Renewed monetary systems that had begun in thirteenth-century Florence and Genoa spread to all of Europe as commerce escalated during the Renaissance and Age of Discovery. Banking evolved and coinage circulated freely once again in Europe. The commercial realities of the old East and new West brought Europe fully out of the Dark Ages. Mathematical literacy took on importance again as the societies of Western Europe matured into economic world centers. Dennis Richardson gives us a hint of the financial atmosphere of Europe in the early seventeenth century.

> In 1609, the bank of Amsterdam was organized to give the community relief from worn and defaced coins. One function of the bank was to accept for safe keeping in perpetuity gold and silver coins and to make credit transfers from one account to another on written orders.
> Coins were deposited with the bank at a discount of 5 percent, and the depositor was charged a service fee of ten florins to cover the costs of opening his account.[32]

Obviously, those who led a comfortable life were fluent in the language of investing, which was written in mathematics.

*   *   *

Literacy was advanced in the West with the invention of the printing press. This wonderful machine made books plentiful and inexpensive, in contrast to the mediæval period, when books were rare and expensive. It was the first time that Greek thought could be read, debated, and analyzed by an evergrowing literate population.

By the mid-sixteenth century, the Polish astronomer, Nicolaus Copernicus (1473-1543) had refuted Aristotle (384 B.C.-322 B.C.) and Ptolemy (85 A.D.-165 A.D.) by advancing the heliocentric (sun centered) view as opposed to their geocentric (earth centered) view of the solar system. Mathematics was also advancing at a respectable pace. John Napier (1550-1617), a Scot, is credited with the invention of logarithms. You may remember studying logarithms if you had Algebra II in high school or college mathematics. However, if you're like most of the well-educated people I have spoken to, logarithms mean absolutely nothing to you!

Logarithms are a convenient mathematical device that eases computations with large numbers by transforming multiplication and division into addition and subtraction. They can also be used to "linearize" nonlinear relationships. Few people had use for logarithms in the seventeenth century. But those who did, such as Johann Kepler (1571-1630) and Isaac Newton (1642-1727), helped to speed along the scientific and mathematical revolutions that have altered how we live and what we need to know.

The Scientific Revolution would not have been possible without the scientific method. Whether we realize it or not, the scientific method has become a part of the way we think. When we hear something remarkable, we usually ask that the statement be supported with facts. Facts, however, are based on observations, and depending on the situation, experimentation. Today, even to the darkest mind, experimentation has value. On the other hand, the typical Medieval person would not have valued the process of experimentation as you or I do. We have been indoctrinated to verify; the process used to do this is the scientific method—formulating a problem and using experimental techniques to come to a conclusion. It is the method that Galileo Galilei (1564-1642) established as the cornerstone of his research and which every other rational thinker has used since.

Even when the results seem incredible, we believe in the truth of scientific results because of the scientific method. Consider the theories of Einstein. Unless you have taken a physics course, you probably do not know what his Special or General Theories of Relativity state. Yet most people see Einstein as a twentieth century icon for science. Why? Because the scientific community tells us that his theories yield correct results when applied to real-world problems.

One of the reasons Einstein's work has such a mystique, is that it violates our common sense view of the world. Einstein tells us that space and time are not absolute quantities. According to Einstein, every time we travel in our car, we begin to age more slowly, increase our mass, and shrink in the direction of motion we are moving in— relative to someone sitting by the side of the road. But the only way to notice these effects is to move unimaginably fast. We would have to accelerate to an appreciable percentage of the speed of light, 186,000 miles per second, in order to detect these changes without sophisticated machinery.

Scientists have conducted experiments with particles which have so little mass they can be accelerated to 99 percent of the speed of light. These experiments verify that the particle's mass has increased and its "life span" is longer. Some particles "live" for only a fraction of a second before decaying into other particles. Measuring the time for a particle to decay when it is at rest relative to us, as opposed to when it is moving at a velocity close to light, shows a time difference in the decay rates.

Another experiment, also showing the effects of "time dilation,"(the slowing of time) uses an atomic clock. Atomic clocks are incredibly accurate devices that use the frequency of atomic vibrations to measure time. They lose no more than one second in a million years. This clock is placed aboard a high speed jet and an identical clock that is synchronous with the clock on the jet remains on the ground. When the jet returns the two clocks are out of sync, the clock on the jet reading behind the clock on the ground, by just the amount Einstein's theory predicts. Hundreds of experiments like these have been performed since Einstein published his Special Theory of Relativity in 1905, and each one has verified the theory. As a matter of fact, scientists could not explain their results or carry on other experiments if they did not use Einstein's theories.

*   *   *

On the coattails of the Scientific Revolution was the Industrial

Revolution. With the advent of mechanization, Western Europe and the United States shifted from basically an agrarian to urban life style. A new social class developed—the wage earner; with him came the time clock, personal income taxes, and the birth of the modern consumer. Numeracy became essential, not a luxury reserved for the well-to-do. Seventh-grade mathematics was finally in everyone's hands.

In the early twentieth century it was algebra, geometry, and trigonometry that separated those who were headed for white collar jobs from those who needed only "business math." Such lines of separation are always fuzzy and many self-made millionaires have been clever enough to prosper without algebra. It will be rare, however, to find millionaires in the twenty-first century not exposed to calculus. Mathematics, in many respects, is becoming the new language for humanity. Social, political, and economic forces are compelling us to become more numerate.

In prior centuries the focus of mathematics was outward; its purpose was to explain the universe. Today we are turning it upon ourselves, gathering data on mass human behavior, trying to understanding how we function, and what we will require in the future.

It has only been within the last two centuries that participatory government has embraced large populations. The growing demand for an educated and numerate society is imperative in an age where people must decide which direction the world will take on the issues of environment, universal health care, species extinction, free trade agreements, foreign aid, population control, nuclear proliferation, and devastating diseases such as AIDS. These problems have a quantitative component that cannot be ignored.

Only by understanding the consequences of our actions, can we change our world for the better. Mathematics can help us see where we are going and what is possible. The responsibility of then acting on those possibilities rests with our political and social will.

CHAPTER FOUR

Numbers for the Nineties

Numbers have the power to evoke an incredible array of feelings in people. Some take on very personal and emotional qualities, such as the date we were born, the date we marry, and the date a loved one dies. Such events form a chronology of life, tucked securely away in mind and heart, shaped by time and number. They offer emotional anchors and guideposts within the flow of time. We navigate through life with the passing decades: "Remember the sixties? I hated the seventies. How about the booming eighties? What do you think the nineties will be like?"

Ten year increments may be an appropriate scale to measure a lifetime, but the stepladder for much of literature and history is centuries. Expressions like The "Nineteenth-Century Novel" and "The Space-Age Twentieth Century" allow us to catalog social, political, and historical change. But historical events do not fall neatly into prearranged time slots ending in zeros. Circumstance, history, and nature have their own internal clocks; they do not abide by our preoccupation with zero years. For whatever the reasons, it is we, not nature, who have organized and characterized personal and historical time by decades and centuries.

Many religious fanatics measure time by the millennium. In 1240 A.D. many Jews and Christians believed the Messiah was on his way, or on his way again. Twelve-forty is not a millennium year you say? True, but it just so happens that 1240 A.D. corresponded to the Jewish year 5000—and we all know the importance zero plays at the end of a year, especially three of them![1]

Geologically, a century is not much different than a millennium. Geologists measure time in tens of thousands of centuries and events are seen from the perspective of epochs and periods. Millions of years can pass before a few feet of sediment is deposited on the ocean floor. Nature has her own time scale, slowly turning ancient life into stone and energy.

Paleontologists tell us that over 400 million years separate the first true skeletal organisms from the first recognizable dinosaurs; as far as we know, life extends back at least three billion years. If one considers all the life our planet has given birth to, by comparison, there is little today. Evolution and extinction have been partners in the intricate dance of life and death. Unfortunately, over the last few decades mankind has accelerated the rate of extinctions beyond all prior accounts in human history. We may yet pay a high price for these actions.

Remarkably, biologists have discovered that all mammalian life appears to be ordained to live the same life span. However, using the sun as a time piece gives little insight into the "connectedness" of life. But when it comes to the biological clock, not so. Nature gives each mammal one-billion heart beats.[2] For some, the pace is fast; for others, it beats slowly. It turns out that if you assign an average heart rate of seventy-two beats per minute to a human being, and go on to find the number of beats in a seventy-five year period, the number comes out closer to three-billion beats. The apparent contradiction arises because a seventy-five year life span is a recent phenomenon for humans, brought on predominately by lower mortality rates due to improved sanitation conditions and advances in medical science. In the "wild", Homo sapiens have an average life expectancy of twenty-five to thirty years, as do many in poorer countries.[3] This brings the number of human heart beats into the one-billion range.

Astronomers tell us similar things about stars. Those which are blue-white burn their nuclear fuel much faster than their cooler yellow and red counterparts. Yet after each converts ten percent of its hydrogen into helium, it strays off what astronomers call the "main sequence."[4] Main-sequence stars are in a state of equilibrium, balancing their outward thermonuclear pressure against gravity's contracting force while fusing hydrogen. The sun and most other stars, at their present stage of stellar development, are on the main sequence. After a star leaves the main sequence it may "live" for many years, but its ability to nurture life as we know it is faint. Would it be too fanciful to liken hydrogen to heart beats?

The universe may be ten to twenty billion years old. Our sun, having converted five percent of its hydrogen to helium is believed to be five billion years old. In another five billion years it will stray off the main sequence and all earthly life will end. Perhaps such information suffers too much detachment from our day-to-day concerns. On the other hand, it may serve as an analog in reminding us that our continuance depends upon our environment. There is an implied hierarchy here: When the nature of the sun's "ecology" changes, all life on Earth will end; when the nature of our planet's ecology changes, vast numbers of extinctions can be expected, possibly our own; when we poison our own bodies, we die.

Though the human mind cannot grasp what a million years, let alone a billion years, "feels" like, we have contained them in our mind's eye with ones and zeros. To the ancient Egyptians a million was an uncommon number. Their hieroglyph for it was a human figure in astonishment (*See Figure 3.1, page 26 for a list of Egyptian numerals*). Today we deal in millions, billions, and trillions. They have become, in some sense, our modern version of "1,2,3, many." There are names for numbers higher than a trillion but most people wouldn't know them. Our current economic and social development does not put us beyond the trillion in most cases.

Many people have either forgotten or never knew the definitions for numbers greater than a million. Their enumeration is straight forward, the key being multiplication by a thousand. For example: a thousand thousands (1000 × 1000) is a million (1,000,000). Notice that a million can be made by adding three zeros to a thousand. A

thousand millions (1000 × 1,000,000) is a billion (1,000,000,000).
Notice again, a billion is just a million with three more zeros added
to it. And similarly, a thousand billions (1000 × 1,000,000,000) is a
trillion (1,000,000,000,000). Try to remember them like this:

```
1              000        000        000            000
        one thousand |
           one million                 |
              one billion                      |
                 one trillion                              |
```

All of this is arbitrary. There would be nothing incorrect if a system were invented that assigned new names to large numbers that
were multiples of a hundred, ten thousand, or whatever you like. In
fact, Britian and Germany define their "billion" the same as we define
our trillion.

It is sometimes difficult to imagine just how large thousandfold
changes can be; an example is helpful.

Assigning units of seconds to these Really Big Numbers (RBNs)
gives:

> one thousand seconds
> one million seconds
> one billion seconds
> one trillion seconds

Since there are 60 seconds in a minute and 60 minutes in an hour,
this works out to 60 × 60 (3600) seconds in an hour. Therefore,
1000 seconds is less than an hour. Actually, it is 1000/3600 hours, or
if expressed decimally: .277... hours or 60 minutes × .277... for
16.66...minutes.

For one million seconds we have: 1,000,000/3600 = 277.77...
hours; or, 277.77/24 = 11.57 days, approximately.

Going on to one billion we have: 1,000,000,000/3600 =

277777.77... hours, and again: 277777.77.../24 = 11,574 days or 11,574/365 = 31.71 years.

And finally, if we continue the pattern that has been emerging, we would add three more 7's to the first number in our series of operations: i.e., 277777777.77, this divided by 24 which gives 11,574,000 days (again three more places) and this divided by 365 yields 31,710 years (again three more places than our previous 31.71 years.) How many years would a thousand trillion seconds (a quadrillion seconds) be?

Collecting our results we have:

> one thousand seconds = 16.66... minutes
> one million seconds = 11.57 days
> one billion seconds = 31.71 years
> one trillion seconds = 31,710 years

As anyone can see, growth by thousands is quite substantial.

Developing a feel for RBNs is essential in today's world, especially with regard to the environment, population, production, waste, health care, and government spending and debt. In the decade of the nineties we can expect to read increasingly about the RBNs associated with these topics. It will become more important for us to understand what these numbers represent objectively, as well as subjectively. We must learn to intelligently personalize their meaning. The rest of Chapter Four is devoted to the role RBNs play both directly and indirectly in our lives.

A Hodgepodge of RBNs

World production of cigarettes reached over 5.1 trillion in 1987,[5] with the United States producing 1,215,221,360 pounds of tobacco for a value of $1,929,763,000.[6] The number of cigarettes produced per person in the United States has, however, dropped to levels comparable to the early 1940s—below 3000 per person.[7] Since less people are smoking in America, tobacco companies are peddling their products overseas where health education is less prevalent. (Unfortunately, as of late 1995 there is a noticeable increase in teenage smokers in America.)

Soybean production in the United States in 1987 was 1,838,053,979 bushels, valued at $10,007,455,000.[8] Ninety percent of the soybeans grown in America are used for animal feed, rather than for direct human consumption.[9] A pity, since soybeans are an excellent source of protein and calcium without any of the cholesterol or animal fat.

Soft drink consumption reached 85 billion twelve-ounce servings internationally in 1990.[10] One wonders how much aluminum was used to spread the gospel of carbonation.

Worldwide over 200 billion bottles, plastic cartons, cans, and paper cups are produced and discarded each year.[11] What happens when all the landfills are full?

Over 450 million vehicles have been instrumental in a quarter of a million traffic fatalities a year worldwide.[12] This is about five times the number of U.S. soldiers that died in Vietnam and one-half the number of people that will die of cancer in the U.S. next year.[13] We can look forward to another 250 million cars joining us over the next seventeen years.[14] Can we assume a proportionate number of deaths?

United States consumers throw away 7.5 million televisions each year.[15] I commend this action. Regrettably, they are discarded because of a failure to function, rather than as a sign of good taste.

We are presently eating the bluefin tuna into extinction. There were some 250 million of them in 1970, but in 1990, estimates put their number at 20,000.[16] Fishermen use nets that are miles long that sweep up everything in their path. It appears no price is too high for sushi.

In 1991 the U.S. produced close to 20 trillion cubic feet of dry natural gas and 9,000,000 barrels of crude oil per day.[17] A barrel contains 42 gallons (for a total of $9,000,000 \times 42 = 378,000,000$ gallons a day) and we still import roughly one-third of our petroleum.

Americans throw away 135,000,000 tons of garbage every year. This is 270,000,000,000 pounds (2,000 × 135,000,000 = 270,000,000,000) which comes to 1,080 pounds per year for each American (270,000,000,000/250,000,000 = 1,080) or nearly 3 pounds per day (1080/365 = 3) for each of us.[18]

There were 19,071,000,000 pounds of chicken consumed in the United States in 1991. Assuming a population of 250,000,000 Americans gives an average of over 76 pounds (19,071,000,000/250,000,000 = 76) of chicken consumed per person.[19] Many people would be surprised to learn that ounce for ounce the average cholesterol content of chicken is no different than red meat. Roasted light meat chicken without skin has more cholesterol than an equivalent amount of broiled sirloin or salami.[20]

Twelve percent of the adult population of the United States is functionally illiterate with skills at or below a fourth-grade level. Try a rough calculation on your own to find a reasonable figure for the number of adult illiterates in America.[21]

The RBNs of Population and Food Production

Another important RBN is population growth. Population does not grow linearly—few things do. Linear growth appears as a straight line when plotted on a graph. (One example of a linear graph is Figure 7.4 on page 129.) Linear means that the rate of growth is constant. For example, if each year you are given a $2000 raise, your salary grows linearly. If the ingredients of a recipe can be doubled, tripled, quadrupled, ... in order to serve two, three, and four times as many, ... then it too is linear. (I am told this is often not the case.)

It took from the dawn of human existence until 1801 for the human population to reach the 1 billion mark.[22] One hundred and twenty-four years later (1925) it had doubled to two billion. (See Chapter 8, page 168, Figure 8.6 for the rise of population in both the First and Third Worlds. The trend noted in the Third World exemplifies the rapid population growth we are currently discussing.)

Successive years for the population growth are cited below:

Year	Population in Billions
1959	3
1974	4
1986	5
1997	6 (predicted)

Notice how the time change is not uniform though the population change is; this is a sure sign of nonlinearity. Population growth is said to grow exponentially—a concept we will explore in detail in Chapter Eight.

Populations in many areas of the world are growing far too rapidly.[23] Over 14 million children (age 5 and under) die preventable deaths every year[24] yet there are over 141 million born each year to replace them.[25] Millions more die every year of malnutrition and disease. The overwhelming number of these births and deaths belongs to the 1.1 billion people who live in the ever worsening Third World.[26] (The term "Third World," though meant originally for those countries not aligned with the U.S. or Soviet Union, has become synonymous for developing or poor countries. Similarly, the term "First World" is used for industrially developed or wealthy nations.) Roughly a third of the people in the Third World are slowly starving to death.[27] By the year 2000, seven-hundred and fifty million people will be without an adequate water supply.[28] Unless there is an abrupt moral, social, and political change, these numbers will continue to rise, making the world even more ecologically and politically unstable.

There is an equal number (1.1 billion) of people in the First World—North America, Japan, and developed Western democracies. We in the First World use the vast majority of the world's resources, though we represent a minority of the population. In terms of food, for example, the waste is tremendous. It is sadly ironic to watch an American family sit down to a dinner of pot roast or chicken, with their heads bowed, giving thanks.

Animal food is highly inefficient to produce, in that it takes many pounds of grain to produce one pound of edible meat. Beef is the greatest offender and poultry the least, which is still considerable. The grain fed to "farm animals" could nominally (in the right political and economic environment) be given to starving people instead. According to John Robbins, seven people could be fed with the grain and soy used to produce the meat, poultry, and dairy products consumed by only one American.[29] A little arithmetic shows that this amounts to 1.75 billion people (250,000,000 Americans × 7 = 1,750,000,000). Such comments are not meant to foster international hand-outs nor are they a necessity. Frances Moore Lappe helped put this in perspective when she wrote:

> Consider Japan and Western Europe, which together contain only one-sixth the population of the poor world. They import 20 times more grain than all the underdeveloped nations combined!
>
> It is our disproportionate use and waste of the world food supply that pushes the price of grain up beyond the reach of those with genuine needs and ensures that the real 'scarcities' appear elsewhere.[30]

The real villain is waste, not scarcity. First World consumption is highly inefficient and politically hazardous to the Third World—which may eventually become hazardous to us. When it comes to diet, First World waste and pollution are mind-boggling. The amount of grains and soy used in producing just 14 percent of our meat-centered diet could sustain nearly 250 million people—our present population.[31] This assumes a linear model, which is the simplest, and most suspect, of all extrapolations. The 14 percent figure works out quickly, if you divide our present population (250,000,000) by the total number of persons (1,750,000,000) that can be fed with the grain and soy given to livestock. (Don't forget to multiply by 100, your answer should read 14.28%; percentage concepts will be covered in depth in Chapter Five.) Could the incredible amount of pesticides, herbicides, and chemical fertilizers that go into our air, land, and rivers to support our present diet be drastically reduced if the focal point of our diets were shifted from animal to plant foods?

To date, 260,000,000 acres of forested land have been cleared to create cropland, pastureland, and rangeland to produce a meat-centered diet.[32] We could return 204,000,000 of these acres to forest and have plenty of cropland available to produce all the food Americans need.[33] This could mean a reduction in farm associated pollutants and toxins by as much as 78 percent. This figure is arrived at by assuming a linear model and computing 204,000,000/260,000,000 × 100. Additionally, over half of all water used in this country is for livestock production.[34] When everything is added up, one-third of all the raw materials (base products of forestry, farming, and mining—including fossil fuels) consumed in the United States is used for the production of livestock.[35]

Carbon Dioxide—an Unlikely Danger

If we were to take a trip back in time, before the emergence of plant-life on Earth, we would find little oxygen to breathe. Plants made the world habitable for us. They converted much of the carbon dioxide in the atmosphere into oxygen. In a sense, plants terraformed the world for humans. They went on to provide us with food, and over millions of years, slowly created the fossil fuels that society depends upon today. How ironic that those ancient plants are now returning our atmosphere back into its primeval state.

As we continue to burn fossil fuels and hack away at the Earth's forests, the amount of carbon dioxide increases. According to frozen samples within Antarctic ice cores, carbon dioxide levels have risen from 280 parts-per-million (ppm) in 1750 (the onset of the industrial revolution) to 330 ppm today.[36] Along with ozone, methane, and chlorofluorocarbons (CFCs), carbon dioxide is commonly known as a greenhouse gas.

Greenhouse gases are so named, because they perform the same function as the glass of a greenhouse. Certain frequencies of sunlight enter unhindered through the glass of a greenhouse. The sunlight is absorbed by the greenhouse contents and re-emitted at a lower energy level (infrared radiation) which cannot breach the glass barrier. The infrared radiation heats up the greenhouse, as sunlight continues to be absorbed. At night, the trapped heat makes its way through the glass by conduction. Unless the outside temperature falls low enough, the conduction process will not equalize the two temperatures by morning. Without a dense enough atmosphere and molecules capable of blocking infrared heat from escaping into outer space, our planet's temperature would plunge each night to levels ill-suited for life. Too much of a good thing, however, can be deadly. Venus, our nearest planetary neighbor in space, has a dense atmosphere made mostly of carbon dioxide. Temperatures at its surface reach 800° F and the sun is never seen through the cloud cover. Its atmosphere acts like a huge greenhouse keeping in a significant amount of the solar radiation that enters. A rise in greenhouse gases on Earth could have disastrous ecological, social, and political effects.

Humanity presently spews over 13 trillion pounds (13,000,000,000,000) of carbon, in the form of carbon dioxide, into the atmosphere each year. This amounts to over 412,000 pounds of carbon every second. The burning of fossil fuels and continued deforestation are mostly to blame.[37] Many scientists believe the Earth has begun a warming trend due to increased carbon emissions, as well as other compounds, that are carrying the Earth's natural greenhouse properties to dangerous levels. Seven of the hottest years on record for more than a century have occurred since 1981.[38] If global temperatures rose only a few degrees Fahrenheit, low-lying communities would be submerged under melting ice from polar regions, leaving a significant portion of humanity homeless. In the United States alone, some 53 percent of the population (about 133,000,000 people) live within a fifty mile strip along our coasts.[39]

Weather patterns could also change, possibly causing one-third of the American Midwest's cropland to whither.[40] We must act quickly in reducing the amount of greenhouse gases expelled into the atmosphere. Estimates by many world experts project that by the year 2020, world temperatures will be on average 1.3° C warmer. An increase of 2° C would push the Earth's average temperature to what it was 125,000 years ago.[41] We have no idea what the overall effects of such changes will bring. Reforestation, fuel efficiency, alternative sources of energy, and conservation, must all be understood for the parts they can play in helping to alleviate this potential problem.

The RBNs of Extinction

By the year 2000, a million species may be driven to extinction. Never in human history has the world been depleted of life at such a rate. Prior to mankind's emergence, the Earth experienced great numbers of extinctions, and always with extreme consequences. When the biosphere's equilibrium is upset, some life forms, sometimes very successful ones, lose heavily; the extinction of the dinosaur and the emergence of mammals is a prime example.

The most popular theory for the disappearance of the dinosaur is extraterrestrial. Most scientists now believe that the Earth was impacted by a large meteorite, which hurled enormous amounts of dust into the atmosphere diminishing sunlight and consequently reducing vegetation. The larger creatures died off and those smaller distant relatives of ours had the upper hand when the dust cleared.

The massive extinctions we are experiencing today have nothing to do with outer space. Mankind is burning down tropical rainforests to raise "cash" crops and cheap beef. Though only 6 percent of the planet is covered with tropical rainforests, at least 50 percent of all species reside there.[42] At current rates, we may eliminate some 15 percent (15 out of every 100) of the world's species between 1990 and 2020. Estimates are hard to come by, because the number of species on our planet is believed to be anywhere from three to thirty million.[43] Many will be gone before we are able to know of them. In the "genocide" that occurs, we may lose plant life capable of strengthening the genetic make-up of our basic food crops.

Common varieties of food, such as corn, wheat, or rice, are sometimes not hardy enough to fend off a disease that is killing it. Scientists rely on wild plants that have not been cultivated, in order to engineer a new strain to fend off the disease. Without sufficient biological diversity, disease and changes in soil or temperature can put an end to our cultivated foods. In recent years scientists have crossbred beans, corn, and tomatoes with wild varieties found in Mexico, Central America, and South America.[44] The importance of biodiversity cannot be overstated. Consider a quote from Vice President Gore:

> It is virtually impossible to calculate the value of maintaining the rich diversity of genetic resources on earth. And indeed, their value cannot be measured by money alone. But where food crops are concerned, we at least have some yardsticks with which to approximate the value of genes that are now endangered. The California Agricultural Lands Project (CALP) recently reported that the Department of Agriculture searched through all 6,500 known varieties of barley and finally located a single Ethiopian barley plant that now protects the entire $160 million California barley crop from yellow dwarf virus.[45]

It is not the $160 million dollars that should stand out here, California's Gross State Product (GSP) is over half a trillion dollars.[46] There is too much at stake to continue practices that imperil our food supply. Specifically, the destruction of our virgin forests both in the tropics and at home.

Many of the wonder drugs of tomorrow may be waiting within tropical rainforests. Curare and the rosy periwinkle are two such examples. The former is used as a muscle relaxant during anesthesia, the latter for treating Hodgkin's disease and childhood leukemia. Both substances originated in tropical rainforests. One-fourth of the prescription drugs used in the United States today are derived from rainforest products, yet only one percent (one out of every hundred) of the plant-life in the tropics has been studied for medicinal use.[47] Presently, humanity is converting rainforest into desert at the rate of over forty million acres a year—an area the size of the state of Washington, and the rate increases every year. This is a sad but important example of nonlinearity. The average loss of rainforest from 1976 through 1980 was about 22 million acres. However, from 1981 through 1990 the average loss was 40 million acres.[48] Using the average amount of rainforest destroyed for the period between 1976 and 1980 would give an expected rainforest loss of 220 million acres from 1981-1990 (22,000,000 acres/year × 10 years). The actual number is 400,000,000 acres (40,000,000 acres/year × 10 years).

Projections based on simple linear extrapolations can make the extinction of the rainforests a problem of the far distant future. Understanding the dynamics of nonlinearity—being literate enough to associate the mathematics with reality—can help gain popular support for ensuing problems well before their catastrophic unfolding.

Health Care, NASA, and the Military

Our health care system serves as another example of RBNs. The total spent in 1992 for all health care was projected to be $817 billion. Of this total, a Consumer Reports article of July 1992 states that at least $200 billion of this is waste.

> Of the $817-billion projected to be spent on health care this year, about one fifth—$163-billion—will go for administrative costs. Except for a fraction of a percent spent on research, the rest—roughly $650-billion—will go to actual patient care. Physician and hospital services together make up most of that total, with the rest going to dentists, nursing homes, drugs, and various other expenses.
> By our estimates, at least 20 percent of that $650-billion, or $130-billion, will be spent on procedures and services that are clearly unnecessary. ... If overuse of medical services wastes $130-billion a

year, administrative inefficiency adds about $70-billion.[49]

The article goes on to say that by changing our current method of health care, we could insure every person in the United States without any increase in cost. We also find out, not surprisingly, that hospital rooms and physicians salaries have far exceeded the Consumer Price Index. (The CPI measures the cost of basic commodities.) As a matter of fact, health care now represents a larger percentage of our GNP than what is spent on our military and public education combined.[50] You would think for all this money we would rate better than twentieth in infant mortality among the industrial nations of the world.[51]

RBNs can be misleading at times. For example, complaints often emerge by government representatives and numerous private citizens to cut government programs that do not appear to have a pressing purpose. One that is usually cited is NASA. The typical argument involves spending the money "down here on Earth" where it is needed rather than in outer space. Not only does this form of shortsightedness attack a worthy program, it displays an unfortunate level of ignorance about the relative level of funding for government programs.

NASA cost the American public about $15 billion in 1992. Yes, this is a lot of money—to have in your bank account, but not when it's evenly distributed in everyone's bank account! Considering that there are a quarter-billion people in the United States, and one-quarter goes into fifteen 60 times, this amounts to sixty dollars per person or two-hundred forty dollars a year for a family of four. A $15 billion investment in NASA more than pays for itself in space age medical breakthroughs and high technology innovations. Future industries and economic opportunities may be found in the spin-off technologies of the aerospace industry. The space program of the 1960s was, in many ways, a catalyst for the electronics revolution. Recall that the waste alone in our health care system may be at least $200 billion. That's over thirteen NASA programs ($200 billion/$15 billion =

13.33..). Or more properly, such waste could finance NASA at its present allotment (neglecting inflation) for the next thirteen years. Some fast arithmetic shows that a family of four pays $3200 ($240 × 13.33... = $3200) a year to finance the inefficiency in our health care system; now that's something to gripe about!

The public often complains about military spending. The Pentagon's budget for 1993 is $294 billion.[52] Assuming the figures in Consumer Reports are accurate, the amount of waste in our health care system could finance over 68 percent of our national defense ($200 billion/$294 billion × 100 = 68%).

A New Orleans Times-Picayune, February 3, 1993, headline read: "'Defensive' care costing patients billions each year." "Defensive care" is taken to mean those procedures (x-rays, CAT scans, etc.) that a doctor will order for a patient, even if he knows they are probably superfluous, to protect himself from a possible law suit. Since most of these expenses are covered by private insurance or federal programs (Medicare, Medicaid) doctors don't consider the costs involved. It's not like the "old days" when the doctor knew the money came out of his patient's pocket and would only recommend tests that he felt were absolutely necessary. Nor is it like the "old days" when it comes to the paranoia surrounding medical malpractice suits.

The article went on to explain that savings could reach as high as $76 billion over a five year period "if doctors and hospitals were freed of malpractice liability and there was a 'no-fault' system similar to workers' compensation." This works out to be $15.2 billion a year in savings ($76 billion/5 years = $15.2 billion/year)—about NASA's 1992 budget. The president of the Association of Trial Lawyers of America referred to the potential savings as "a drop in the health-care bucket that would be wiped out by cost increases in two months." Obviously, pricey malpractice cases are not a "drop in the bucket" when it comes to a lawyer's annual earnings.

When it comes to money on a governmental scale, perhaps Senator Everett Dirksen summed it up best when he said, "A billion here, a billion there and pretty soon you're talking about real money."

Whether we deal with health care, funding for NASA, or military spending, it is imperative to see the larger picture. Dollar amounts must be seen in perspective. Isolated figures, without proper comparisons, are elements of deception. Mathematics taken out of context is at best useless, and at worst, potentially fatal.

The National Debt

Our national debt increases by $13,000 each second.[53] In early 1993, the American people suffered from a national debt of over 4 trillion dollars ($4,000,000,000,000). A majority of this debt (80%) we owe to ourselves, the rest (20%) we owe to foreigners.[54] Don't think for a moment that since we owe a substantial portion of the debt to ourselves it is not too serious—unless, of course, you're willing to toss away your savings bonds, life insurance policies, private pension plans, or the interest on your bank accounts.

Our government has run deficits throughout its history. But it wasn't until the 1980s that we started to run deficits that are considered high for a peace-time economy. During the 1980s the United States increased defense spending while cutting taxes. "Trickle-down" economics was supposed to encourage corporations to invest and expand, thereby boosting the economy, which in turn would "trickle-down" to people like you and me in terms of goods and jobs. Regrettably, most corporations used their tax savings to engage in mergers and buy-outs, thus creating more debt than anything else. Additionally, wealthier individuals took advantage of lower personal income taxes, as well as a reduction in capital gains taxes, and speculated in the stock market. Such actions leave less money in circulation for real investments and give a false sense of worth to market holdings. And finally, increased government spending in concert with tax cuts, helped to create huge revenue short-falls, or more commonly, big deficits.

Projections for 1993 put the national debt at over 60 percent of our Gross National Product (GNP).[55] This means over 60 percent (more than sixty cents out of every dollar) of what we produce is obligated for debt. At the present rate of debt accumulation, our debt will equal the GNP within seven years.[56] The United States has not had a ratio of debt to GNP this high since World War II. However, the postwar trend (1946 to 1981) showed a strong, healthy decrease. (See Figure 7.10 in Chapter Seven page 143.) This ratio slowly started to pick up momentum and further accelerated during the 1980s. Unless something is quickly done, these numbers will escalate to values indicative of a state of national emergency.

In order to finance the deficit, each year the federal government must borrow money. Government does this by selling securities—saving bonds, Treasury notes, and Treasury bills. The government must offer competitive interest rates to attract would-be buyers. A buyer could be an individual who purchases a $25 savings bond or an investment house that buys millions of dollars worth of Treasury bills. With competitive interest rates and very low risk, both Americans and foreigners purchase these securities. (Those who wish higher interest rates must go into the private sector where greater rewards mean greater risks.) But the government sells only one thing—debt. Buying government securities helps the government pay down their present debt while creating future debt. But every dollar that goes into government securities is another dollar unable to be recycled into industry and business, where real money and higher standards of living are made.

What if every person in America took all their savings and bought United States Savings Bonds in an effort to pay down the present debt? Since all of the nation's savings was going to pay off debt, none would be left in commercial banks to give small business loans, home repair loans, mortgages, etc.. To a much lesser degree, this is what occurs when the government competes with private institutions for the public's money. Less money is available to the private sector, which means loans are harder to get and interest rates rise because the money supply is smaller. A chain reaction then occurs, wherein business becomes more expensive to conduct, which translates into cut backs and layoffs. Since the economy is doing poorly, less taxes will be collected (and more people will become dependent on the state) which means the estimated deficit for that year will be even larger. The government is now straddled with less revenue, rising costs, and rising interest payments, and an escalating debt—and the cycle continues. The net effect of this process is to magnify the national debt—**which is the sum of all past deficits**. Paying off debt by creating new debt is not wise.

Consider the following example: Let's say a salesman does poorly for the year and needs to borrow $5000 to cover his expenses. He is charged 20 percent interest per year, which means a maximum pay back of $6000 if the loan is paid back within one year. (The $6000 is computed by first computing 20 percent of $5000 and then adding the principle of $5000. Note: 20 percent of $5000 is the same as one-fifth of $5000.) The salesman must therefore earn his normal salary, plus an additional $6000 during the next year. If he suffers another bad year he will be forced to borrow again. The **cumulative** money he will then owe (principal and interest) is analogous to the national debt. The money he needs to borrow at the end of the year to pay creditors is analogous to the deficit. If America, like the salesman, continues to live like this, the country will eventually be borrowing money just to pay off the accumulated interest.

The federal government had a $75 million debt in George Washington's time and now wrestles with a $4 trillion debt.[57] (An argument can be made that comparing dollar amounts over a two hundred year period is meaningless without a consideration of social and economic factors. Though this is absolutely correct, the intention here is only to emphasize a numerical change by a factor of over 53,000!) You can't really appreciate the increase in the debt unless you understand how millions and trillions are related. Do you know how many millions make a trillion? (Try to figure it out on your own. The question, however, is answered in the next chapter.)

The national debt should worry us, since each American has the burden of paying for it. Try this calculation: There are approximately

250,000,000 people in the United States today. If the national debt is
four trillion dollars, how much does this equal for each man, woman,
and child?

How much for a family of four? We will return to these questions
in Chapter Five. Too often we carry the same incorrect mind-set into
the real world that we had in school. Namely, "Don't bore me with
the details, just give me the answer." We, as taxpayers, need to understand the dynamics and numbers involved in the economic follies of
some politicians. When public officials tell us that deregulation will
do so and so, we must demand a balance sheet showing how all those
wonderful numbers are achieved. We needed to see the master plan
for Reaganomics and President Clinton's economic reform package in
black and white. When President Reagan asked in 1984: "Are you
better off today than you were four years ago?", the proper response
should have been, "Perhaps, but at what cost and where will we be
ten, fifteen, or twenty years from now?"

In a front page New Orleans Times-Picayune article of February
10, 1993, titled "Clinton orders deep cuts in White House staff, pay"
we find that these "cuts" will save $10 million. The 1993 deficit is
projected to be $327 billion. How much of a savings are we talking
about here? Proportionately speaking, it would mean that a person
earning $25,000 a year could expect to save 76 cents (see Chapter
Five, problem 5, page 82). If your family was on hard times, would
you call a family meeting to tell them you had devised a plan to save
76 cents a year? Would it be front page news? Clearly, the president's
effort to cut expenses, and hence reduce the deficit, is at best symbolic. Families on hard times need to create a mind-set that trims every
corner possible. But the real solution lies in cutting large, inefficient
expenditures and raising appropriate revenues. In other words, cutting the fat from many programs and increasing taxes (in one form or
another). There is no other realistic way to make ends meet and pay
off our debt.

My point is not to diminish the value of saving even a million dollars; it is to show the contrast between the amount of waste that is

accepted, versus meager cut backs and the lack of funding for vital programs that is astounding. (Head Start is a good example of a federal program that works, but has never been funded enough to provide for all children.)

There is nothing esoteric about computing budgets. Most of the mathematics would not go beyond seventh grade arithmetic and it could be explained in reasonable language, if the "master plan" was really understood by those espousing it. True, there is no way for the government to predict what next year's economic climate will be like; no more than a merchant can predict exactly how much he will earn. The government is also at a greater disadvantage, in that it must earmark money for programs sometimes years in advance. But there is no reason the possible risks and assumptions involved in such planning should not be presented to, and understood by, the public. This is where a cogent public education has its greatest currency. People would have a greater appreciation (and comfort range) of such matters, if there was practical meaning attached to mathematics training in school. Curricula needs to be based on the problems that students will be confronted with—not determining how many nickels and dimes Joe has in his pocket, or the fact that he will be twice his son's age in four years. If real problem solving skills were taught in school, the public would demand more than qualitative arguments and hand waving from those who set policy. Teaching with a meaningful context has a rich dividend for society. Real education helps to maintain a focus on real issues. This is the kind of training that should be carried into voting booths across America.

* * *

In the past chapter we have briefly covered some of the more important issues facing us in the nineties and no doubt in the next century. Most of the writing has been qualitative so the reader could become familiar with these problems without being bogged down with mathematics. Chapter Five will begin the quantitative work, with references back to many of the topics already discussed.

CHAPTER FIVE

Nuts and Bolts

C reating a clear and concise notational system is the first step in formulating more useful mathematics. In sharp contrast to this are the number systems of ancient societies which were ill-suited for even simple multiplication and division. A good notational system can be compared to a fine musical instrument. Both the musical instrument and the notational system hold incredible potential and yield amazing results in the right hands. The key in both instances is exploration and imagination.

Playing with Pieces—A Look at Fractions

Below are four interpretations of fractions:

1. A fraction represents a part of something, or a whole plus a part of something. For example, ¾ is a part of something while ⁴⁄₃ is a whole plus a part.

2. A fraction represents division. Since we freely used a / to represent ÷ in Chapter Four this must come as no surprise. For example, ¾ = .75; the denominator is divided into the numerator (bottom number into top number) to find the "decimal equivalent" for a given fraction.

3. A fraction represents the product of a whole number and a unit fraction. Three-fourths is equivalent to $3 \times \frac{1}{4}$ ($\frac{3}{4} = 3 \times \frac{1}{4}$).

4. Any fraction can be thought of as a ratio. (¾ can mean, 3 compared to 4, or 3:4.)

Of all the different ways to write fractions, the third one in the list on the previous page is the most difficult for people to understand. Ironically, it also offers one of the most insightful views of fractions.

Any fraction can be expressed as a whole number times a unit fraction—where a unit fraction has 1 in the numerator such as ½ or ⅕. The fraction ¾ can be rewritten as the whole number 3 times the unit fraction ¼ (3 × ¼). Think about what ¾ represents—three one-fourths. Similarly, 5/6 represents five one-sixths. What does three twos mean? You could write this as 2,2,2 or 2 + 2 + 2 or 2 × 3. The harder to understand fraction concept works the same way. Three-fourths can be thought of as ¼,¼,¼ or ¼ + ¼ + ¼ or 3 times ¼ (3 × ¼). Furthermore, if the phrase, "three twos" is taken to mean, three sets of two, or two sets of three, then 3 × ¼ can be interpreted as 3 sets of ¼ or ¼ of a set of 3. But notice what happens when we word it this last way (¼ of a set of 3). One-fourth of a set of three, is some part of three. We're taking a part of something, but that sounds like division. But we're multiplying! We know we are multiplying because if we say it in reverse, three sets of one-fourth, we see the additive principle we associate with multiplication. Since 3 × ¼ is no different than ¼ × 3 (just as 2 × 3 = 3 × 2) it must mean both statements are equivalent. Therefore, multiplication by fractions is equivalent to division. If we wished to, we could eliminate the traditional concept of division and replace it with multiplication (though I don't advise it). Perhaps we should also replace the word "multiplication" because it gives the misleading notion of a purely "increasing" process, which is certainly not true when multiplying with fractions.

Decomposing a fraction into a whole number times a unit fraction also offers insight for the rule governing multiplication with fractions. Since 3 is the same as 3⁄1, then 3 × ¼ is the same as 3⁄1 × ¼ which we know is ¾. The most immediate way to arrive at this answer is to multiply across, that is, 3 × 1 over 1 × 4, which is ¾. The same process is true for any numbers, for example:

$\frac{3}{8} \times \frac{5}{7} = (3\times5)/(8\times7) = \frac{15}{56}$

Some of the people who missed the multiplication problem with fractions on my survey (see Chapter Two) tried to multiply the numerators and add the denominators. Such attempts show no understanding of the concept of multiplication with fractions. Let's work with the previous problem to show the rule for multiplication in a slightly different way than we did using ¾.

We can write ⅜ × 5/7 in various ways by using unit fractions, and the fact that the order of multiplication is irrelevant. We have:

(3 × ⅛) × (5 × 1/7) = (3 × 5) × (⅛ × 1/7), which immediately shows that the numbers in the numerator must be multiplied together. A similar argument for multiplying 8 × 7 in the denominator can be used as was done for ³⁄₁ × ¼. It is better though, to try and develop a "feel" for why this operation yields reasonable results. Remember, ⅛ × 1/7 can be thought of as a one-eighth part of one-seventh. Visualize taking a seventh of a piece of pie, and then taking one-eighth of this small piece. In other words: What size piece of pie will we have if a seventh of a piece of pie is cut into eight pieces? Since there are seven, one-seventh pieces in a pie, and each seventh is cut into eight pieces this makes for a total of 8 × 7 tiny pieces. Therefore, if the total pie is cut into 56 pieces, than one piece is 1/56 of the pie.

This is a tremendous amount of work to try to show the logic (not proof) of fraction multiplication, namely a/b × c/d = (a × c)/(b × d). The real value in all this arithmetic is to make the reader aware of how to manipulate fractions in this manner.

We could also view the problem ⅜ × 5/7 as three-eighths of a set of five-sevenths. Visualize what this statement is saying by approximating. We are taking nearly one-half (⅜) of nearly three-quarters (5/7). Which is like taking one-half of 75 cents or about 38 cents or ³⁸⁄₁₀₀ of a dollar. How close is the approximation to the actual answer? The decimal equivalent of ¹⁵⁄₅₆ is about .27 (divide 56 into 15) or ²⁷⁄₁₀₀. Even though our quick approximation is off a fair amount, our answer is not ridiculous. This is important because it lends support to our view of multiplication with fractions as taking a part of something, or in this case, taking a part of a part.

One of the major stumbling blocks for students enrolled in algebra (perhaps a better name for algebra is symbolic arithmetic) is that they don't understand basic operations with fractions. Many algebraic manipulations depend on the general statement $a/b = a \times 1/b$. Yet students as far along as trigonometry are often unable to apply this concept.

In Chapter One I discussed division of fractions. Recall that none of the middle school teachers I asked understood why inverting and multiplying gave the correct answer for dividing two fractions. The rationale for this rule hinges on using the number 1 in a creative way. Any number (other than zero) divided by itself is equal to one. That is: $5/5$ or $.7/.7$ or $(3/4) / (3/4)$ are all 1. Furthermore, multiplication by one leaves a number unchanged. That is: 5×1, $.7 \times 1$, or $3/4 \times 1$, all remain 5, .7, and $3/4$.

Now consider the division problem $3/8 \div 5/7$. This can be rewritten as $(3/8) / (5/7)$. If we multiply the fraction $3/8$ over $5/7$ by 1, we still have the same fraction. But what if we express "1" as $7/5$ over $7/5$ and multiply this by $3/8$ over $5/7$. We have: $(3/8) / (5/7) \times (7/5) / (7/5)$, which is, $(3/8 \times 7/5)/(5/7 \times 7/5)$. The denominator multiplies out to 1, and we are left with the numerator which is itself the multiplication problem $3/8 \times 7/5$. This is what we have if we invert and multiply. The rule "invert and multiply" comes from answering the question: By what number must the bottom fraction be multiplied to reduce to one? This number is the "reverse" (the proper term is inverse or reciprocal) of the bottom fraction. The number 1 is then expressed as this reversed number divided by itself, and multiplied with the original problem. Hence, division is turned into multiplication, by multiplication with "1".

In Chapter Three, I briefly discussed addition of fractions. The important concept here is to make sure likes are added to likes. In order to add $1/3$ and $1/5$ we must have a "standard" by which both fractions can be compared. The usual rule is to find the "least common denominator" for both 3 and 5. This is the smallest number both 3 and 5 will evenly divide into, which in this case is 15. We can re-express $\frac{1}{3}$ and $\frac{1}{5}$ in terms of fifteenths by again imaginatively using the number 1. If $\frac{1}{3}$ is multiplied with $\frac{5}{5}$, and $\frac{1}{5}$ is multiplied with $\frac{3}{3}$, the results are $\frac{5}{15}$ and $\frac{3}{15}$ which totals $\frac{8}{15}$. One difficulty with adding fractions is that the least common denominator is not always easy for people to discern. In cases where the least common denominator is not readily apparent, it can easily be avoided. The only important consideration for adding fractions is to make sure all the denominators are the same number. What if we had completely ignored the question of a least common denominator when we were adding $\frac{1}{3}$ and $\frac{1}{5}$ and just quickly sought any number that would make both denominators equal. Let's say we quickly notice that 3×10 and 5×6 are both 30 and decide to transform both denominators into 30. To do so, we multiply $\frac{1}{3}$ with $\frac{10}{10}$ and 1/5 with $\frac{6}{6}$. This gives $\frac{10}{30}$ and $\frac{6}{30}$ which added together gives $\frac{16}{30}$. But $\frac{16}{30}$ can be reduced since $16 = 8 \times 2$ and $30 = 15 \times 2$. Therefore, $(8 \times 2)/(15 \times 2) = 8/15 \times 2/2$ which is 8/15. It may, at times, be easier to forget about finding a least common denominator and use any number that will give equal denominators. Then, after the problem is worked, it can be put in lowest terms.

* * *

Fractions are not as simple, nor are the "rules" governing their operations, as obvious as many authors of mathematics books would have us believe. Operations with whole numbers border on the intuitive for most people, but the same cannot be said for fractions. It is for this reason that ancient societies, as well as current college graduates, have had difficulties with the subject.

Percentage

One of the more startling revelations of my study was that one out of four persons could not compute eight percent of six dollars, yet percentages are used in most professions and in many daily transactions. They are used to compute federal, state, and city taxes. They are present when buying, and selling, and tipping. Merchants use them to lure customers to buy their wares by announcing "40 percent off the retail price." Batting averages, bank loans, salary increases, and grades on tests are all stated with percentages. Everyone should know what percentages represent and how to work with them.

Percentages, when one is comfortable with them, immediately provide for a sense of proportion. Which is easier to visualize, $5/7$ of a pie or a little over 71 percent? Percentages are based on one-hundred. So 71 percent is the same as 71 pennies out of one hundred pennies, which is more easily understood than $5/7$ of one hundred pennies.

For the purpose of computing with money, 8 percent is seen as 8 cents on every dollar (eight pennies out of one hundred pennies). Eight percent of two dollars is 16 cents because each dollar represents 8 cents. Therefore, 8 percent of $6.00 is $6 \times 8¢ = 48¢$. Similarly, 15 percent is 15 cents on a dollar. Fifteen percent of $6.00 is $6 \times 15¢ =$ 90¢. To find the 8 percent sales tax on $6.50 only requires determining 8 percent of 50¢, since 8 percent of 6 dollars is already known. The appropriate question is: If 8 percent means 8 cents for each dollar, how many cents for only half of a dollar? Since 50¢ is half of one dollar (100 pennies) then the tax should be half as great, or 4¢. Likewise, since there are four 25 cent units in a dollar, each 25 cents must have 2¢ of the eight cent burden upon it.

So 8 percent of $6.50 is: $(6 \times 8¢) + 4¢ = 52¢$
Similarly, 8 percent of $6.25 is: $(6 \times 8¢) + 2¢ = 50¢$
What is 8 percent of $6.75?

The above line of reasoning will always work, but it is slow and cumbersome. A more illuminating pattern is needed.

We already have determined that 8 percent of $6.50 is 52 cents. Notice what happens when $6.50 is multiplied by 8:

$6.50 \times 8 = $52.00

Obviously, fifty-two dollars cannot be the answer, but the fifty-two is correct; it's only a matter of where the decimal point is placed. If the decimal point were moved two places to the left, this would give $.52 (fifty-two cents). But moving a decimal point two places to the left corresponds with division by 100, or multiplication by $\frac{1}{100}$. If the problem had originally been written as $6.50 × 8 × $\frac{1}{100}$ or $6.50 × .08, fifty-two cents would immediately follow.

The above suggests a rule: **To compute using a percentage, drop the percent sign (%) from the number, then place the number over 100, express decimally and multiply.** This "rule" should come as no surprise, since the concept of percentage is based upon 100.

Consider the following example: Find 15 percent of $56.87.

15% = $\frac{15}{100}$ = .15
$56.87 × .15 = $8.53

What if, however, we are given any fraction and asked to express it as an equivalent percentage? Consider the fraction ¾. If the 4 is divided into the 3 the result is .75, so ¾ and .75 mean the same thing. If the rule for turning a percent into a decimal is internally consistent, then the reverse—turning a decimal into a percent should be: **Multiply the decimal by 100 and then put in the percent sign.**

Thus, .75 x 100 = 75%

This implies that fractions, which are convertible to decimals (by dividing the denominator into the numerator) must also represent percentages. It must be that 3/4 is equivalent to 75 percent. Any fraction is therefore equivalent to a percentage, and hence, expressible with respect to one-hundred.

Find the equivalent percentage for $\frac{60}{250}$, and rewrite it with respect to one-hundred.

$\frac{60}{250}$ = .24 (by dividing 250 into 60)

Converting to a percentage: .24 × 100 = 24%

Since all percentages are based on a hundred we have:

$^{60}\!/_{250} = {}^{24}\!/_{100}.$

This tells us that 60 is related to 250 the same way 24 is related to 100. So a pie cut into 250 pieces, will be about one-fourth consumed when 60 pieces have been eaten.

As a final example, we will look at the ratio of the national debt to the Gross National Product (GNP). Earlier it was stated that the national debt has increased from $75 million to $4 trillion since the founding of the United States. Though the national debt has apparently grown substantially over the years, the dollar figures by themselves are not very revealing. Without a more objective measure, there is no way to understand what the changing debt represents. Though many factors should be considered to develop an accurate picture of America's rising debt, considerable insight can still be glimpsed by the simple ratio of debt to GNP.

A ratio (fraction) can be regarded as a comparison of top number to bottom number. Calculating this ratio for 1981 and 1992 will give an absolute measure of how our debt has risen with respect to our production over this eleven year period. (The larger the span of time used, the less meaningful the comparison becomes, since so many more variables—energy requirements, education, recreation, etc.— are introduced. Hence, a comparison of this ratio over a two hundred year period would be rather meaningless.)

This ratio (percentage) went from 33.3% in 1981 to 67.2% in 1992.[1] In absolute terms, this means that for each one-hundred 1981 dollars of the GNP, $33.30 was already committed to debt. Eleven years later, out of every one-hundred 1992 dollars, $67.20 was debted.

Just as an individual has less money for daily cost of living expenses when burdened with debt, so too does government.

The following examples are provided to reinforce concepts involving percentages.

Examples

1. If you earned $30,000 last year and paid $8,400 in taxes, what percent of your income did you give Uncle Sam?

In computing percentages, it is always important to ask yourself: What is being compared to what? Or: What is the part and what is the whole? In this example the whole is $30,000, so the ratio is: 8400/30000 = .28, .28 × 100 = 28%.

2. Out of every one-hundred dollars earned in the above example, how much is left to the taxpayer?

Since 28% means 28 out of one-hundred, what remains is 72 dollars, per each hundred earned.

3. You pay $50.00 for an item and sell it for $125.00, what was your profit in dollars and what percentage is this?

In dollars: $125.00 − $50.00 = $75.00 profit.
Percentage: $75.00/$50.00 = 1.25, 1.25 × 100 = 125%. (Percentage of profit is defined as: (profit in dollars/cost to seller) times 100.) See Appendix A for an alternative definition.

Example number 3 should make it clear that fractions, ratios, and percentages can be greater than 1, or equivalently greater than 100 percent. It can be misleading to think part/whole when the "part" can at times be larger than the "whole". To avoid this confusion, clarify exactly **what** is being referenced to **what**. Think more along the lines of **compared amount/base amount**. In example three, the profit was compared to the cost. There is no reason it could not have been reversed.

4. It was stated previously that 67.2 percent of the GNP in 1992 was tied to the debt. Approximate the GNP for 1992.

Since we wish an approximation, we can take advantage of the fact that 67.2% is very close to 66.66 ... % which is an easy fraction to work with, namely ⅔, which yields a repeating decimal, (66.66 ... % = 66.66 ... /100 = ⅔.) Therefore, the ratio of debt to GNP is about 2:3. Since the debt is approximately $4 trillion we write:

4/? = ⅔, by observation, ⁴⁄₆ reduces to ⅔, so the GNP must have been approximately $6 trillion for 1992.

Lastly, we show how the result on page 70 in Chapter Four was calculated.

> 5.) How much would a person have to save out of an annual salary of $25,000, if the proportion was to be the same as for a $10 million savings out of $327 billion?

Since $10 million out of $327 billion was saved, we have: $10,000,000/$327,000,000,000 = 1/32,700 = .00003058. Therefore, $25,000 × .00003058 = 76¢.

Powers of Ten and Scientific Notation

In the past, RBNs were cumbersome to work with because of their size. Multiplication and division with such numbers were slow and tedious. Today, calculators manipulate RBNs with ease, but in doing so, often resort to a mathematical shorthand called scientific notation. The study of scientific notation is dependent on yet something more fundamental, called "powers of ten" notation.

Numbers such as 10, 100, 1000, 10000,. . ., can all be expressed as products of ten times itself. That is, ten is simply 10, one-hundred is 10 × 10, one-thousand is 10 × 10 × 10, ten-thousand is 10 × 10 × 10 × 10, and so on. Instead of writing all these zeros a shorthand notation is employed:

$$100 = 10^2$$
$$1,000 = 10^3$$
$$10,000 = 10^4$$
$$100,000 = 10^5$$

$$1,000,000 = 10^6$$
$$1,000,000,000 = 10^9$$
$$1,000,000,000,000 = 10^{12}$$

Note that the numeral written above the zero of ten (called an exponent) corresponds to the number of zeros in the original number.

A million, billion, and trillion can now be expressed as:

$$10^6 = \text{one million}$$
$$10^9 = \text{one billion}$$
$$10^{12} = \text{one trillion}$$

In general, each time the exponent increases by three, a new name is given for the number, for example: 10^{15} is called a quadrillion and 10^{18} is called a quintillion.

The Universal Almanac gives names for numbers up to 10^{33} (a decillion) and then jumps to 10^{100} which is given the name googol and finally $10^{10^{100}}$ which is called a googolplex. Often, metric prefixes are assigned to these numbers. The term megabyte, used with computers, means 10^6 (a million) bytes. (A byte represents the information from eight "data lines" that are represented by a series of ones and zeros, called bits.) Other common metric prefixes are: giga is 10^9 (a billion), tera is 10^{12} (a trillion), peta is 10^{15} (a quadrillion), and exa is 10^{18} (a quintillion). As stated earlier, numbers beyond a trillion are not generally encountered, except in scientific literature, and those that are, usually are stated only as a power of ten without regard for prefixes.

Numbers such as 10^2 and 10^3 are sometimes referred to as ten squared and ten cubed, respectively. Larger numbers, such as 10^4 are generally read as "ten to the fourth" or "ten raised to the fourth power."

Some of the numbers quoted in Chapter Four are restated below:

1. The four trillion dollar deficit: $\$4 \times 10^{12}$.

2. The eight hundred seventeen billion dollars for health care: 817×10^9.

3. The present world population of five billion three hundred million people on Earth: 5.3×10^8.

4. The four hundred fifty million motor vehicles: 450×10^6.

There is only a small step required in going from powers of ten to scientific notation: **Numbers written in scientific notation are expressed as a number between one and ten which is multiplied by the appropriate power of ten.** In the examples given above, only the first and third are already in scientific notation. In order to see how to express numbers in scientific notation, we must first explore some of the properties involving powers of ten notation.

We begin by multiplying 100×1000; this yields 100,000. Rewriting the problem in powers of ten gives: $10^2 \times 10^3$. Since one-hundred thousand can also be expressed as 10^5 we can then write $10^2 \times 10^3 = 10^5$. (Remember that the exponent represents the number of zeros.)

How about $10^3 \times 10^4$? This is $1,000 \times 10,000$ which equals 10,000,000. So $10^3 \times 10^4$ must be 10^7. Much of the success (and pleasure) in learning mathematics rests on seeing patterns. Consider the two examples just presented:

$$10^2 \times 10^3 = 10^5$$
$$10^3 \times 10^4 = 10^7$$

Do you see any possible relationship with the exponents in each case?

A good guess would be: When multiplying powers of ten, add the exponents of the two tens on the left and use this sum for the exponent on the right. We can test this idea by taking other examples. If our guess is correct, then $10^6 \times 10^6$ should be 10^{12} (since $6 + 6 = 12$). Recall that 10^6 is a million and 10^{12} is a trillion (see above list). Does one million times one million equal a trillion? It certainly does.

Therefore, to answer a question asked in Chapter Four, it takes a million millions to equal one trillion. A trillion is truly a **Really Big Number!**

Generalizing these results for any exponents a and b gives: $10^a \times 10^b = 10^{a+b}$.

We are now ready to tackle scientific notation. Consider the dollar amount cited for health care on page 64. In order to express 817 as a number between one and ten (which, as cited earlier, is a requirement for scientific notation) we write it as 8.17×10^2. **The exponent of ten, is now more generally understood as representing the number of places the decimal point is moved.** Since 817 has an implicit decimal point after the 7, it is rewritten as 8.17 by moving the decimal point two places to the left, and then compensating by multiplying this smaller number with ten raised to the appropriate power $(8.17 \times 10^2 = 8.17 \times 100 = 817.)$ We can now express 817×10^9 as $8.17 \times 10^2 \times 10^9 = 8.17 \times 10^{11}$ (since we know $10^2 \times 10^9 = 10^{11}$). Similarly, in example four, 450×10^6, can be restated in scientific notation as $4.5 \times 10^2 \times 10^6$ which equals 4.5×10^8.

Scientific Notation has yet another advantage. The value for the tobacco crop given in the last chapter was $1,929,763,000. There is a degree of ambiguity concerning the three zeros on the end of this number. Are we to assume this was exactly the value of the crop, or that the figure was rounded to the nearest thousand dollars? Considering that numbers in the real world don't usually work out so evenly, the dollar value cited is probably an approximation valid to the nearest thousand dollars. To show this using scientific notation, the number is written as 1.929763×10^9, where the three zeros are not included. On the other hand, if the value is exact to the dollar, the figure is written as 1.929763000×10^9. This tells the reader the zeros are, to use the correct phrase, "significant figures", rather than place holders used for an approximation.

Try this example: On average, each person's share of the national debt is $16,000. If there are 250 million people in the United States what is the total debt owed?

Using scientific notation we have: $1.6 × 10^4$ per person × 2.5 × 10^8 people. This can be rewritten as ($1.6 × 2.5$) × ($10^4 × 10^8$) which equals $4.0 × 10^{12}$. The reverse of this question was asked on page 70 and the answer should have been $16,000.

RBNs are divided as well as multiplied. We therefore need to investigate the properties of our notational system for division.

Consider   the   two   expressions   10,000/100,   and 100,000,000/1,000, which are equal to 100 and 100,000, respectively. Rewriting with powers of ten gives:

$$10^4/10^2 = 10^2$$
$$10^8/10^3 = 10^5$$

Can a simplifying rule (a recognizable pattern) for division be postulated?

Notice that if the exponent of the bottom number is subtracted from the exponent in the top number, this yields the exponent in the answer. Other examples would continue to support this process. Generalizing this pattern for any exponents a and b gives: $10^a/10^b = 10^{a-b}$

In 1950, world oil production was roughly ten million barrels per day. The United States, alone, uses more than this today. If there are, to the nearest power of ten, approximately one hundred thousand seconds in a day, about how many barrels of oil were produced in 1950 per second, on average?

10^7 barrels/10^5 seconds = 10^2 barrels/second or
100 barrels/second

Let's make the previous problem regarding the amount of money owed by each person on the national debt a division problem. This will now be the same problem asked on page 70. Using scientific notation the problem is written:

($4 × 10^{12}$)/($2.5 × 10^8$) people = ($4/2.5$) × ($10^{12}/10^8$) = $1.6 × 10^4$ per person, where 4/2.5 is treated as one calculation and $10^{12}/10^8$ as another.

I have purposely not yet stated values for 10^0 or 10^1, since I have found they often confuse students. We will begin with 10^1 first. Since $10^2 = 100$ it would be correct to guess that $10^1 = 10$. A convincing demonstration of this is the statement $10^1 \times 10^1 = 10^2$. The exponent on the right must equal the sum of the exponents on the left, so it follows that each exponent on the left must have a power of one since $1 + 1 = 2$.

Lastly, we turn to 10^0. Does this mean anything or are we pushing the notation beyond its usefulness? Consider the problem 100/100 or $10^2/10^2$. The answer is 1. Returning to the rule for division, we find the answer is 10^{2-2}, which is 10^0. The implication is that 1 and 10^0 are the same thing. This is true for any number raised to the zero power, **because the zero power signifies a number divided by itself.**

Whenever a number takes the form 10^a, the 10 is called the base. Everything we have discussed is applicable for any base. In other words, $5^3 = 5 \times 5 \times 5$, $4^1 = 4$, $9^0 = 1$, $7^5/7^2 = 7^3$, and so on. Ten was chosen for its simplicity; since multiplication by tens is just a matter of counting zeros.

Negative Exponents

There is still another aspect to dividing powers of ten that must be addressed. What does the problem $10^3/10^5$ mean?

Rewriting the problem as: 1,000/100,000 yields an answer of $\frac{1}{100}$. Following the rule discovered for division with exponents gives $10^{3-5} = 10^{-2}$ for the answer. (Recall that when a larger number is subtracted from a smaller number the answer is negative. For example, $20 - 30 = -10$. You can think of a negative number as representing debt—if you owe $30 but have only $20 then you would enter $-$\$10 in your checkbook. Negative numbers are also any numbers to the left of zero on a **number line**—see Figure 7.1 in Chapter Seven page 125 for a description of the number line.) Therefore, 10^{-2} and $\frac{1}{100}$ must equal each other since both are solutions. The same line of reasoning would mean $\frac{100}{1,000,000}$ is 10^{-4}. Is there a recognizable pattern?

$$10^{-2} = \tfrac{1}{100} = \tfrac{1}{10^2}$$
$$10^{-4} = \tfrac{1}{10,000} = \tfrac{1}{10^4}$$

A good guess for a general rule might be: $10^{-a} = \tfrac{1}{10^a}$. You might try a few more examples to convince yourself of this and also try to understand that this "new rule" is not new at all, but a result of the previous rule for division. Elegant notational systems often reveal unexpected results.

Negative exponents are another way to express fractions and decimals. Consider the equality $.007 = 7 \times 10^{-3}$. How was this equality determined? Three "different" views are provided below:

1) $.007 = 7 \times .001$, but $.001 = \tfrac{1}{1000} = \tfrac{1}{10^3} = 10^{-3}$ so we have 7×10^{-3}.
2) $.007 = \tfrac{7}{1000} = 7 \times \tfrac{1}{1000} = 7 \times 10^{-3}$.
3) $.007 = 7 \times 10^{-3}$.

Therefore the -3 exponent means move the decimal point three places to the left. **(Any negative exponent shifts the decimal to the left, just as a positive exponent shifts the decimal to the right.)** Since the 7 in 7×10^{-3} has an implied decimal point (7.) three places over from this would give .007 as required.

Three Examples

1. On average, how many twelve-ounce soft drinks were produced in 1990 for each person on the planet? (Stated another way: What was the per capita twelve-ounce soft drink consumption worldwide in 1990?)

In 1990, eighty-five billion twelve-ounce soft drinks were produced, (see page 56) and there were approximately five billion three hundred million people on the planet.

Therefore:

8.5×10^{10} drinks/5.3×10^9 people = $(8.5/5.3) \times (10^{10}/10^9) = 1.6 \times 10^1$ drinks/person.

For values such as 1.6×10^1, scientific notation is often disregarded and the number is simply written as 16, especially if there is little ambiguity concerning significant numbers as in this case (explained on page 85).

> 2. Livestock production is highly consumptive and polluting. Every second 230,000 pounds of excrement is generated by livestock.[2] How much is this per year?

Since there are 86,400 seconds in one day (60 sec/min $\times$ 60 min/hour $\times$ 24 hours/day = 86,400 sec/day = 8.64×10^4 sec/day), and there are 31.536×10^6 seconds in one year (3.65×10^2 days/year $\times 8.64 \times 10^4$ sec/day = 31.536×10^6 sec/year). This number must be multiplied by 230,000 pounds per second. Therefore: 2.3×10^5 pounds/sec $\times 31.536 \times 10^6$ sec/year = 72.53×10^{11} pounds/year or 7.253×10^{12} pounds/year (7,253,000,000,000 pounds/year, or approximately 7.25 trillion pounds/year). Note, if we are true to significant figures, then 7.25 should be rounded to 7.3 since the 2.3×10^5 pounds/sec has only two significant figures.

> 3.a) If the bluefin tuna had been eaten to extinction in 1970, what would each person's share of tuna have been worldwide?
> b) Same question but for 1990?

a) On page 56 it was stated that there were two hundred fifty million bluefin tuna in 1970. World population in 1970 was three billion seven hundred twenty-one million people.[3] Let's make the assumption that, on average, each fish has 750 pounds of edible flesh. (Bluefins are huge fish, which can live in excess of thirty years and reach a weight of at least 1500 pounds.)[4]

Therefore: $2.5 \times 10^8 \times 7.5 \times 10^2$ pounds/3.721×10^9 people = $(2.5 \times 7.5/3.721) \times 10^{10}/10^9 = 5.04 \times 10^1$ pounds/person, or simply 50.4

pounds per person. (Using only two significant figures we should state the answer as 50 pounds.)

b) In 1990 there were 20,000 bluefin tuna and world population was five billion three hundred seventeen million.[5] For 1990 we have: $2.0 \times 10^4 \times 7.5 \times 10^2$ pounds$/5.317 \times 10^9$ people $= (2 \times 7.5/5.317) \times 10^6/10^9 = 2.82 \times 10^{-3}$. Using two significant figures the answer should be 2.8×10^{-3}. Without scientific notation the answer would be written as: .0028 pounds per person or about .045 ounces per person! In other words, whereas in 1970 each person could have had over 2 ounces of fish every day for a year, today there isn't enough remaining for each person to really know what it tastes like. Indeed, instead of the 2 ounce per day figure for 1970, the 1990 figure is roughly one ten-thousandth of an ounce per day. The above results can be calculated by recalling there are 16 ounces to a pound. Therefore, .0028 pounds × 16 ounces/pound equals **.045** ounces, and 50 pounds × 16 ounces equals **800** ounces. Each number divided by 365 gives the numbers quoted above.

*   *   *

A final note on negative exponents. Just as RBNs are given names, so too with Really Tiny Numbers (RTNs). Using seconds again, we have:

10^{-3} (.001) seconds = 1 millisecond (a thousandth of a second)

10^{-6} (.000001) seconds = 1 microsecond (a millionth of a second)

10^{-9} (.000000001) seconds = 1 nanosecond (a billionth of a second)

10^{-12} (.000000000001) seconds = 1 picosecond (a trillionth of a second)

There is, of course, no limit to RTNs but such numbers lack practical application for most people.

Order of Magnitude

You don't hear many people say, "Last year I earned $25,387.31". More likely, the quoted figure would be $25,000. Rounding off numbers is a useful technique for getting a "feel" for the size of a number, without becoming hampered with exact figures. Sometimes, trying to be too exact can get in the way of creative thinking, where more energy goes into detail than is necessary.

Much of the time we are not interested in exact figures, just a reasonable estimate. (Recall the oil example where we rounded the number of seconds in a day to one hundred thousand.) When the national debt is cited as over four trillion dollars, it is understood the debt is closer to four trillion dollars than five trillion dollars. Ten or twenty million one way or the other is rather insignificant. Remember, a million is only one-millionth of a trillion. Even if we were off by as much as four hundred billion dollars, it would still put us within 10 percent of the correct figure. Often, it is more illuminating and efficient to concentrate on a "power of ten" solution, rather than aiming for an exact answer. The phrase "order of magnitude" is a synonym for power of ten.

The national debt spans 12 orders of magnitude, because a trillion is 10^{12}—the exponent is the order. How many orders of magnitude is a trillion greater than a billion? Three, since a billion is 10^9, and a trillion is 10^{12}. Three orders of magnitude correspond to a factor of a thousand, six orders to a million and nine to a billion. When someone says, "His figures are off by an order of magnitude," they mean he's off by a factor of ten. That's generally significant; it's the difference, for example, between an annual salary of $25,000 versus $250,000.

Enrico Fermi (1901-1954), an Italian-American physicist, was instrumental in developing the atomic bomb during World War II. He also made many peacetime contributions to science and is generally considered one of the most eminent physicists of the twentieth century.

As a teacher, Fermi was known for giving his students problems which initially seemed impossible to solve. Many were of a technical nature. Others, although somewhat trite, were used to illustrate his technique. One famous problem is: How many piano tuners are there in Chicago? Short of going for a phone book, most of us would be at a loss in finding a solution. Fermi, however, was often able to arrive at answers to such questions in a matter of moments without the need of pencil and paper. Such "solutions" are possible because Fermi problems do not demand exact answers. They ask only for reasonable answers, where "reasonable" is defined as having the correct order of magnitude.

Common sense and basic information play a crucial role in all Fermi problems. Before attempting to "solve" the piano tuner problem, consider some "solutions" that are unreasonable.

Would a million (10^6) piano tuners be a reasonable number? No, of course not. How about 10^5 or 10^4? What would you guess for the lowest reasonable order of magnitude? This is certainly no way to arrive at an answer, but it does begin to narrow the possibilities, as well as forcing us to use a common sense approach.

Deciding upon a reasonable population range for Chicago is a necessary first step. A guess of at least one million but no more than ten million is probably sound. If we start with one million, it would then be easy to multiply our final answer by two, three ..., depending on how many millions Chicago actually has.

If Chicago has a million residents, there would be 250,000 families, assuming, on average, four people to a family. Perhaps one family in five has a piano, this amounts to 50,000 pianos (250,000/5). (Implicit in our assumptions are that the number of pianos will supply the demand for some sustainable level of piano tuners.) If one piano tuner can tune, on average, four pianos a day and works 225 days a year (this number allows for weekends, holidays, two weeks vacation, and sick days) then he can tune 900 (4 × 225) or roughly 1000 pianos a year. If pianos are tuned about once every five years then 10,000 need tuning each year (since there are 50,000).

Therefore, (10,000 pianos per year)/(1,000 tunings per tuner) = 10 piano tuners for each one million Chicago residents. Since Chicago's population is closer to three million, this gives 30 piano tuners. From an order of magnitude point of view, the answer is between 10 and 100 (10^1 and 10^2).

Clearly, many of my assumptions could be challenged. But most answers to this problem, for any set of reasonable numbers and assumptions, will be between ten and one-hundred. This is what makes the process valuable. Though the details may never be known with certainty, a plausible and convincing range of values can be determined.

*   *   *

Fractions, percentages, scientific notation, and order of magnitude calculations are all useful in explaining and calculating a wide range of modern day problems. They should not be viewed as isolated concepts, but as a set of elements that can be brought together to deepen understanding. Like musical notes, they each have their own identity, but when combined, they are capable of much greater expression. In the chapter that follows, three problems are examined in great detail which use many of the mathematical concepts we have previously discussed.

CHAPTER SIX

Three Problems — Diet, Inflation, and Taxes

The following problems are designed to help the reader become more familiar with the mathematics discussed in Chapter Five. Each problem provides for more than the one-dimensional view that most math problems are reduced to in high school and college textbooks. The problems are structured so that the mathematics is perceived as an "embedded fragment" (albeit an important fragment) rather than isolated from the information it is illuminating. The reader will find the questions posed to be topical and diverse. Hopefully, this chapter will help readers become more sensitive to the power, necessity, and versatility of mathematics.

Problem #1
Fat from Fiction

By mid-1994 Americans should be seeing a revolution in food labeling. The Nutrition Labeling and Education Act authorized the Food and Drug Administration (FDA) to create a meaningful and simple labeling system for all processed foods. At first glance, such news may seem minor compared to inflation and taxes. But what we eat is intimately tied to our economy, our environment, and our health. The decade of the nineties will set the stage for large scale shifts in dietary patterns that will redefine our preferences and our consumption.

Over the last five to ten years Americans have grown more con-

cerned with the associated risks of heart disease and cancer due to the
Standard American Diet (SAD), which has traditionally consisted of
high-fat, low-fiber foods.

All of us were taught in school to eat a diet based on the four food
groups. The first two groups are composed of meat and dairy products which are high in fat and low in fiber. If you're like most
Americans, you remember those colorful charts used by your teachers
to show the benefits of an animal food diet. All of these materials
were provided free to our schools by those who had the most to gain
by the consumption of these products. The National Dairy Council
and the Beef Council are examples of industries that have spent millions of dollars to bring us the virtues of animal products. We never
realized we were being handed a sales pitch instead of sound nutri-
tional advice.

After World War II, animal product consumption rose dramatically in America.

There are several reasons for this:

1. Americans became more affluent and could afford eating higher
on the food chain.
2. Grain production rose to high surplus levels, due to chemical
innovations with fertilizers and pesticides. Therefore, it made sense
economically to feed the surplus grain to animals, especially cows,
because they ate the most and gave back the least.
3. The rise of agribusiness and the development of factory farming
emerged. (Factory farming has little to do with farming in the traditional sense. It is a concentrated form of husbandry where tens of
thousands of animals are kept in confined areas. The advent of
strong antibiotics made intensive confinement possible. Without
these drugs, such "farms" would be lost to epidemics of disease.)
4. The meat and dairy industries sold the public on the idea that
animal products were indispensable to human health.

Studies over the past thirty years have indicated that a high-fat,
low-fiber diet (which is usually a meat-centered diet) is not as healthy
as those in the medical profession and food industry once pro-

claimed. One study conducted in the early 1970s showed a strong correlation between fat consumption and breast cancer.[1]

Accurate food labeling is the first line of defense for consumer health and for controlling the enormous cost of health care that every American shoulders through private funds and tax dollars. How much of a tax burden would be lifted from all of us if the incidence of expensive degenerative diseases such as cancer and heart disease were substantially reduced? John Robbins devoted a large portion of his book, *Diet for a New America* to the cause of preventative medicine. I have taken the liberty to quote a rather long passage from his book:

> Billions upon billions of dollars are being poured into the search for the 'magic bullet' that will cure cancer, a search that has thus far been utterly unsuccessful. And yet, at the same time, another search has been underway which has borne great fruit. Unbeknownst to the public, we have been learning more and more about how to prevent the disease in the first place.
>
> The tragedy is that the American people have been continually cajoled into putting their trust and their money into the thus-far-futile search for a cure, and have not been told what has been learned about prevention. Without this information, Americans every day unknowingly choose to eat foods that contribute heavily to their risk of cancer.
>
> In 1976, the United States Senate Select Committee on Nutrition and Human Needs, under the chairmanship of Senator George McGovern, convened public hearings on the health effects of the modern American diet. After listening to the testimony of the nation's leading cancer experts, McGovern was not particularly delighted with the war on cancer, calling it a 'multi-billion dollar medical failure.'
>
> At one point in the proceedings, McGovern pointedly asked National Cancer Institute director Arthur Upton how many cancers are caused by diet. The head of the largest cancer organization in the world replied 'up to 50 percent.'
>
> McGovern was dumbfounded. 'How can you assert the vital relationship between diet and cancer,' he demanded, 'and then sub-

mit a preliminary budget that only allocates a little more than one percent (of the National Cancer Institute funds) to this problem?'

Dr. Upton responded sheepishly: 'That question is one which I am indeed concerned about myself.'

The problem is that diet is not a 'magic bullet.' It is a way of preventing cancer, but only in rare cases a way of cure. Organizations like the National Cancer Institute are not encouraged to focus much attention on prevention because there is vastly more money to be made in treatment, and far more glamour in the possibility, however remote, of a cure. Attention is further drawn away from prevention by food industries whose products are known to be involved. They apply immense pressure on government and public health organizations to keep them from informing the public as to what is known about dietary prevention. The result is that you and I are continually being told to put our faith and our money into cancer treatment, and into the hope for an eventual cure. We are not told how to keep cancer from happening in the first place.

The tragic result is that we are losing a war we could prevent.[2]

The new food labeling was fought by meat producers because fat consumption guidelines were originally designed to be based on a 2000 calorie diet, of which no more than 30 percent of the calories were derived from fat. Since meat is high in fat, and fat is high in calories, a 2000 calorie diet provides for only modest meat consumption. A compromise was finally reached with the meat industry wherein two diet scenarios will appear in 1994 on food labels: one for a 2000 calorie diet and another for a 2500 calorie diet.[3]

Since there have never been any guidelines set by law, fat percentages have often been computed based on the weight of a serving size. Producers of high fat foods can make some of the fattiest foods appear a delight to dieters by referencing their calculations to weight. But a little thought will show this method to be lean on meaning and fat on deception.

All living things depend on food for their survival. Those who produce high-fat foods would have us believe it is the weight of the food we consume, rather than the energy it provides, which is essential. But anyone with common sense can see energy, not weight, is the issue—it's **what** is eaten that counts, not **how much.** You choose: four pounds of apples a day for the rest of your life, or one to two pounds a day of varied foods. Take whole milk for example: An 8 ounce serving has a "weight" of 226.8 grams (grams are really a measure of mass not weight). Only 9 grams are fat. So fat as a percentage of weight is:

$9/226.8 \times 100 = 3.97\%$, which is low (4% assuming only one significant figure). To avoid any confusion all answers will be given to two significant figures unless otherwise stated.

A more meaningful calculation, however, is fat as a percentage of calories. An 8 ounce serving of whole milk has 150 calories. One gram of fat has 9 calories. Since there are 9 grams of fat, this gives a total of 9 grams $\times$ 9 calories/gram = 81 calories. The percentage of fat from calories is: $81/150 \times 100 = 54\%$, which is close to fourteen times greater than the previous answer.

Computing the percentage of fat from total calories is exactly the information you and I need to know to make healthy decisions. If 50 percent of our available energy is in the form of fat, the risk of heart disease and cancer is substantially higher. The present government guideline recommends no more than 30 percent of calories from fat, and there are those in the medical profession who advocate numbers as low as 20 and even 10 percent.[4]

Even maintaining a diet with as much as 30 percent fat from calories will require Americans to reduce their consumption of animal foods appreciably. This, as cited above, has caused the meat industry much concern, which is why they lobbied against nutrition labeling. A higher caloric diet, however, allows for a higher level of fat consumption.

As stated previously, the new food labels will have guidelines for two diet scenarios, they will be:

1. A diet based on 2000 calories per day, where no more than 30 percent of the calories are derived from fat.
2. A diet based on 2500 calories per day, where no more than 30

percent of the calories are derived from fat.

The important questions for us to ask are:

If one gram of fat has 9 calories, how many grams of fat can be eaten without exceeding the 30 percent limit, given a 2000 calorie diet and a 2500 calorie diet?

Thirty percent of 2000 calories represents the total number of fat calories permitted each day. This number divided by 9 calories per gram gives the number of grams of fat that can be eaten each day.

Thus: 2000 calories × .30 = 600 calories,
   600 calories/9 calories per gram = 66.67 grams

Most labels presently give the number of grams of fat per serving so it is only necessary to add up your daily total and keep it under 67 grams.

A diet based on 2500 calories per day gives:

2500 calories × .30 = 750 calories,
   750 calories/9 calories per gram = 83 grams.

The new labels will also give the percentage of fat in a serving, based on 2000 calories per day. For example, if a serving has 13 grams of fat, this represents 20 percent of your total fat intake for the day (13/66.67 × 100 = 20%). Additionally, the label will provide the number of calories in a serving and the number of calories from fat. This will be yet another measure of fat content. The above item may have 260 calories a serving, of which 120 are from fat. This tells us that the item, though providing only 20 percent of our fat intake for the day (120/600 × 100 = 20%), is itself 46 percent fat (120/260 × 100 = 46%). In addition to the total fat, both saturated fat and cholesterol content will be listed on food labels in 1994.

Most saturated fat is found in animal products, with the exception of some tropical oils, but only in animal products do we find cholesterol. In dairy products, fat and cholesterol are usually found together. Thus, many low fat items are also lower in cholesterol. This, however, is not true of meat products where cholesterol is found predominately in muscle. Lean cuts of meat, therefore, do not affect cholesterol content. Most people erroneously assume that only red meat poses a cholesterol problem. Ounce for ounce, the cholesterol content of chicken is comparable to that of red meat. The only way to reduce cholesterol consumption is to eat less animal products.

Atherosclerosis, a warning sign for heart attacks, results when cholesterol occurs in plaques along the inner walls of the coronary arteries, closing off the flow of blood to our heart. Low-density lipoprotein (LDL) is commonly called "bad cholesterol," because of its role in transporting two-thirds of all cholesterol through our circulatory system. Much of this cholesterol ends up adhering to the inner walls of our blood vessels. (The body also has high-density lipoprotein (HDL) which is supposed to remove the accumulating cholesterol from blood vessels, hence it is referred to as "good cholesterol.") Since saturated fats are found with cholesterol, most medical authorities advise reducing saturated fats to no more than 10 percent of our daily calories, as well as keeping daily cholesterol consumption to within 300 milligrams.[5] (A milligram (mg) is a thousandth of a gram.) Before leaving Problem #1, try the two exercises below:

> 1. Louis Rich Turkey Bologna is advertised as 90 percent fat free—10 percent fat. A one ounce serving (28 grams) = 1 slice. Fat content is 3 grams and one serving has a total of 45 calories.
> a) Compute the percentage of fat by weight and the percentage of calories from fat. (Recall 1 gram of fat has 9 calories.)

Answers: 10.7 percent by weight and 60 percent from calories

Note—All numbers shown on food labels have been rounded-off. Do not expect computed values based on these numbers to yield consistent results for the total calories printed on the label. When computing the total calories, 4 calories per gram for protein and carbohydrates is used, as is 9 calories for one gram of fat—but these figures are also approximated. For example, Kellogg's Nutri-Grain Almond Raisin Cereal has 140 calories per serving. The label lists 3 grams of protein, 31 grams of carbohydrates, and 2 grams of fat. Since both protein and carbohydrates have the same number of calories per gram, we have: (3+31) × 4 = 136 calories + 2 × 9 = 18 calories for a total of 154 calories. This is not necessarily an attempt to distort the facts (especially in this example, since a smaller number of calories per serving would appear to increase the percentage of fat in each serving), but it is an example of mathematical confusion. Most companies provide a toll free number on their labels for consumer questions.

> b) Assuming a maximum of 67 grams of fat per day, what percentage of total calories from fat would 4 slices of this bologna provide for the day?

Answer: 18 percent

> 2. A "brown bag" lunch is packed for your child that contains two bologna and American processed cheese sandwiches, each spread with a tablespoon of butter. The sandwiches have one slice of bologna (Louis Rich Turkey Bologna) and one slice of American cheese. One slice of American cheese has 8.9 grams of fat and 106 total calories. One tablespoon of butter has 10.8 grams of fat and 101 total calories.[6]
> a) Compute the percentages of fat calories for cheese and butter.

Answers: cheese — 76 percent, butter — 96 percent

Again, due to rounding-off, the answer for butter did not evaluate to 100%. Actually, butter has a very small amount of carbohydrates .06 grams per tablespoon, so it is not entirely fat, but close enough.[7]

> b) Compute the total number of grams of fat eaten for lunch.

Answer: 45.4 grams

c) What percentage of the total fat requirement for the day has been consumed? Solve the problem for both a 2000 calorie diet and 2500 calorie diet.

Answers: 68% and 55%

Calculate the above values if a one ounce bag of potato chips and an 8 ounce glass of whole milk are also consumed for lunch. Do you think this lunch is healthy?

Problem #2
Inflation—or How to Compare Apples to Oranges

An article in the Investor's Business Daily (February 18, 1993) titled "Clinton's New War on Drugs" defended drug price increases and the role drug companies play in supporting our economy and lessening hospital costs. The author maintained that government regulation is one of the reasons for higher priced drugs. The focal point of this argument centered around legislation passed in the early 1960s.

In 1962, the Kefauver Amendments (named after Senator Estes Kefauver) were passed. These amendments gave the Food and Drug Administration a greater voice in the approval process for new drugs. The law stated that companies must "prove not only that a new drug was safe—as was required under previous law—but also effective."[8] According to the article, "In 1963, before the law was fully implemented, it took only 2.5 years and $29 million to bring a new drug to market.

By 1990, the drug approval process took 12 years, on average, and more than $231 million ..."[9] It may well be that the drug companies are getting a bum deal by the Clinton Administration, but using the dollar amounts cited above are misleading. The article makes no reference to the effects of inflation for the dollar amounts cited. Comparing "dollars" from different time periods without taking inflation into account is like the proverbial apples to oranges comparison—it makes no sense. Using the figures given above, one concludes the cost to pharmaceutical companies, due to government regulation, has increased by close to a factor of eight ($231/29 = 7.96$). But this calculation ignores time and inflation—$231 million over **12 years** and $29 million over **2.5 years**. The article does not indicate in "what dollars" the quoted amounts are given. Is the $231 million figure referenced to 1990 dollars, or is it a sum of all the money spent (ignoring inflation) twelve years prior to 1990? The value of the dollar changed appreciably during this time period. It turns out that this information ($231 million over a twelve year time period) was taken from "a study by Joseph DiMasi, an economist at the Center for the Study of Drug Development at Tufts University."[10] In an effort to better understand the newspaper quote, I called Joseph DiMasi at Tufts University and asked him exactly how the $231 million was computed. He told me that his study used the time period 1970-1982 and that the $231 million figure was referenced to **1987 dollars**. He was unable to provide any verification of the 1963 figure, as it was not part of his study. Though I'm sure the journalist was sincere in his efforts, not enough information was provided to the reader in the article. Without careful consideration, two erroneous conclusions can quickly be made:

> 1. As stated above, the cost to drug companies appears to have risen nearly eightfold from 1963 to 1990.
> 2. On a yearly basis the cost rose from $11.6 million/year to $19.3 million/year—a price increase of almost twofold. (These figures are obtained by dividing $29 million by 2.5 years, and $231 million by 12 years.)

The central question of Problem #2 is: **How much have costs for drug implementation increased between the early 1960's and the period 1970-1982 in constant 1987 dollars?**

To answer this question we must have an understanding of inflation. Inflation is insidious. Every money civilization has suffered its effects. Recall the problems in ancient Athens discussed in

Chapter Three. Solon's devaluation of Athenian currency was a risky solution to a perilous problem. Remember, when money is devalued its purchasing power declines; this is no different than inflation.

Inflation in America has averaged about 4 percent over the last ten years (1983-1993). That is, if the value of the dollar is referenced to 1983, it has, on average, lost 4 percent of its buying power each year thereafter. For example, if the inflation rate averaged exactly 4 percent each year, we would have: $1.00 × .04 = 4¢; this means a 1984 dollar has the purchasing power of 96¢ with respect to a 1983 dollar. Another 4 percent inflation for 1985 would mean 4 percent off of the "96¢ dollar" of 1984. Since inflation is typically calculated from one year to the next, an average inflation rate of 4 percent over ten years would not devalue a dollar by 40¢; the amount is closer to 31¢. To make this point clear, below is the changing value of a dollar over a ten year period assuming constant 4 percent inflation. (All calculations are rounded to the nearest penny.)

Table 6.1

Decline in purchasing power of a dollar at constant 4 percent inflation

Year	Value of dollar referenced to year 1
1	100¢
2	96¢
3	92¢
4	88¢
5	85¢
6	82¢
7	78¢
8	75¢
9	72¢
10	69¢

Table 6.1 shows that after ten years at constant 4 percent inflation a "tenth year dollar" will only buy 69¢ worth of goods compared to a

"first year dollar." There are many ways to describe this situation:

1. The buying power of the "tenth year dollar" is at 69 percent
($^{69}/_{100}$) of the "first year dollar."
2. The buying power of a dollar has fallen 31 percent (100-69)/100 = $^{31}/_{100}$, over a ten year period.
3. If Table 6.1 is assumed to represent inflation for consumer prices, then you would need $1.44 "tenth year dollars" to have the same purchasing power as one "first year dollar" ($1.00/.69 = $1.44).

An appliance in "year one" costs $1000 and the same appliance costs $1500 dollars in "year ten." It appears the price has increased 50 percent. But 1500 "tenth year dollars" are only 1035 "first year dollars" ($1500 × .69 = $1035). The increase in constant dollars is $35 and therefore: $^{35}/_{1000}$ = .035 or 3.5 percent.

Table 6.2 gives consumer and producer prices in constant 1967 dollars. Since the costs for "producing" new drugs were cited in the newspaper article, this is where our attention will be focused.

Table 6.2

Purchasing power of dollar for producer and consumer prices for 1959-1990 (1967 = $1.00)

Year	Producer Prices	Consumer Prices
1959	1.08	1.15
1960	1.07	1.13
1961	1.07	1.12
1962	1.06	1.11
1963	1.07	1.09
1964	1.06	1.08
1965	1.04	1.06
1966	1.01	1.03
1967	1.00	1.00
1968	0.97	0.96
1969	0.94	0.91

Year	Producer Prices	Consumer Prices
1970	0.91	0.86
1971	0.88	0.82
1972	0.85	0.80
1973	0.78	0.75
1974	0.68	0.68
1975	0.61	0.62
1976	0.59	0.59
1977	0.55	0.55
1978	0.51	0.51
1979	0.46	0.46
1980	0.40	0.41
1981	0.37	0.37
1982	0.36	0.35
1983	0.35	0.34
1984	0.34	0.32
1985	0.34	0.31
1986	0.34	0.30
1987	0.34	0.29
1988	0.33	0.28
1989	0.31	0.27
1990	0.30	0.26

Source: Facts and Figures on Government Finance 1992 Ed.

Based on 1967 dollars, a "dollar" in 1963 had $1.07 worth of purchasing power. Similarly, a 1987 dollar had $.34 worth of purchasing power (see Table 6.2). To answer the original question, one must compute the value retained by a dollar between 1963 and 1987. (We can't be sure to what year the $29 million figure was referenced. But since the value of the dollar was fairly constant during the early 1960s, according to Table 6.2, using the value of the dollar in 1963 is reasonable.) We proceed as follows: $.34/$1.07 = .32 or 32 percent. This means every 1987 dollar is worth only 32¢ compared to each 1963 dollar. Therefore, in 1963 dollars, (231×10^6) 1987 dollars have a value of $.32 \times \$231 \times 10^6 = \$74 \times 10^6$.

So how much has the cost risen to bring a drug to market today as opposed to the early 1960s? There are several ways to answer this question. The increased cost is $74 million - $29 million or $45 million. Or, the cost has increased by a factor of 2.55 since $74 million/$29 million = 2.55. These calculations, however, do not tell the whole story. The element of time must also be considered. In the first case we are talking about 29 million 1963 dollars over 2.5 years, and in the latter case, 74 million 1963 dollars over 12 years. The best way to compare "apples to apples" is to calculate the average cost per year. Twenty-nine million dollars over a 2.5 year period works out to $11.6 million/year ($29 million/2.5 = $11.6 million/year). Likewise, $74 million over 12 years works out to $6.2 million/year ($74 million/12 = $6.2 million/year). This shows that the yearly cost to producers in constant dollars is about half of what they were paying in 1963! This is arrived at by the computation: $6.2 million/11.6 million $\times$ 100 = 53%. The actual cost has fallen by 100% - 53% = 47% on a yearly basis.

Alternatively, the problem can be done from the point of view of constant 1987 dollars. We proceed as follows: If 32¢ in 1963 buys the same amount as a dollar in 1987 then it takes 3.13 1987 dollars to equal one 1963 dollar (1.00/.32 = 3.13). Therefore, $29 million in 1963 is the same as $90.8 million in 1987 ($29 million $\times$ 3.13 = $90.8 million). The cost per year in 1987 dollars is:

$90.8/2.5 = $36.3 million/year for 1963 and
$231/12 = 19.3 million/year for 1987

And just as before the cost per year to drug producers is 53 percent of what it was in the early 1960's (19.3 million/36.3 million $\times$ 100 = 53%).

So which is it? Have drug costs increased or decreased? The answer depends upon how you look at the problem! Which tells us that a little skepticism about the conclusions people reach using numerical information is healthy. If inflation isn't mentioned and dollar figures are quoted for different years, be on your guard. Remember the vital role time can play in interpreting one situation in more than one way. Before leaving "Problem #2", try doing the exercises below:

> 1. A car, comparable to one that cost $6000 in 1980, sells for $12,000 in 1993. (Use Table 6.2 for Consumer Prices, assume the purchasing power of the dollar for 1993 is 23¢.)
> a) What is the cost in constant 1980 dollars?
> b) Using constant dollars, determine the percentage increase in price.

Answers: a) $6732   b) 12%

> 2. Computer power that cost $2000 in 1986 sells for $500 in 1993.
> a) What is the cost in constant 1986 dollars?
> b) How much has the price gone down in 1986 dollars?
> c) By what percentage has the price of computing power gone down from 1986 to 1992?

Answers: a) $383   b) $1617   c) 81%

Note—Using 3 significant figures $1617 should be $1620

Problem #3
A Taxing Situation

President Clinton has proposed an energy tax (as of early 1993) to help offset the federal deficit. The tax would levy an extra 59.9¢ per million BTUs (British Thermal Units) on gasoline and heating oil, and 25.7¢ per million BTUs on natural gas, coal, and nuclear energy.

There is always a flurry in Congress and among the general public over any form of tax increase; understandably, since "tax and spend" is as dangerous as "cut and spend." Regardless, it seems inevitable that the American people will be asked to help pay down the deficit by increased taxes in one form or another. The natural question for most of us is: How much? Though we can never be certain what the final cost will be, the problem below may provide for a good start.

Based on the previous figures, what should the average American expect the President's energy tax to cost if it is implemented?

There is a "fast and dirty" way to get an upper limit on this amount by finding the BTU consumption per capita for the United States. This information can be found in an Almanac or can be easily calculated if not given directly. Most Almanacs give the total number of BTUs used per year in the United States. If the book does not explicitly give the consumption per capita, it can be found by dividing the total consumption in BTUs by the population of the United States. This answer would be very rough since it does not separate out energy use by commerce, industry, and the military. It does, however, bring up an interesting point.

Usually, this kind of tax is based on primary energy expenditures that the average person must pay, such as gasoline for automobiles and home energy fuel. However, since every product that is sold depends on energy for its creation and relies on energy to bring it to market, producers will no doubt pass on their increased costs to consumers. This part of the tax is hidden from view. Indeed, calculating the tax burden based on per capita energy usage may represent a rough estimate for the **maximum** outlay each American can expect to pay. We will do this, as well as a computation for primary energy expenditures based on gasoline and home fuel use. Computing the cost for the latter, however, requires a bit more effort, since some homes rely on oil and others natural gas.

Before beginning the mathematical part of the work, it would be beneficial to digress for the moment and discuss the concept of energy, since many readers may not understand what a BTU measures.

Measuring Energy

Energy is an abstract concept. It is associated with all things in nature and manifests itself in a myriad of ways. Scientists can measure and use energy, but no one really understands what it is.

It wasn't until well into the nineteenth century that scientists understood that heat is a form of energy. The Englishman James Prescott Joule (1818-1889) showed that mechanical work and heat are equivalent. He did this by attaching a weight on a string that was strung over a pulley and connected to a paddle wheel. This allowed the weight to turn the paddle wheel when released. Before allowing the weight to fall he measured the temperature of the water. After the weight had fallen he measured the temperature again and found an increase due to the frictional effects of the paddle wheel in the water. Knowing the temperature increase and the amount of water in the bucket permitted him to formulate a relationship between mechanical work and heat. Since the temperature increase of the water due to the rotating paddle was indistinguishable from heating the water with a flame, the two processes (mechanical work and heat) were seen as equivalent.

Had scientists initially understood the relationship between work, heat, and energy, there may never have been a reason for calories or BTUs, since both work and heat are a measure of energy. Nor is it only correct to express the energy content of food in calories, it is more a matter of history; food could just as well be represented in BTUs. Historically, both the calorie and BTU were defined by the amount of heat necessary to raise a given amount of water to a fixed temperature. In the case of the calorie, it was defined as the amount of heat needed to raise one gram of water (about a twenty-eighth of an ounce) from 14.5° to 15.5° Celsius. The more common food calorie is called a "big calorie" and is defined as one thousand of the calories described above (1 **kilo**calorie = 1 food calorie). A BTU is similarly defined as the heat necessary to raise one pound of water from 63° to 64° Fahrenheit. The calorie has been used more in laboratory work, whereas the BTU is employed for industrial and engineering needs.

In 1948, scientists honored James Presscott Joule by using his name to represent the standard energy unit in the International System of Units. Presently, the calorie and BTU are being phased out because their definitions are now viewed as archaic. Work, heat, and energy are increasingly being expressed in Joules today.

The Joule is not a fundamental unit of measurement. It owes its definition to the product of force and distance. One Joule is the amount of energy required when a force of one Newton acts over a distance of one meter. A Newton is a unit of force or weight in the metric system; one pound equals 4.45 Newtons and a meter is about 39 inches. Therefore, lifting a weight of slightly less than a quarter-pound a distance of 39 inches off the ground requires one Joule of energy. The energy released in burning one wooden match is about one BTU; this in turn is equal to 1,055 Joules (written as 1055 J). Clearly, a Joule is a small unit of measurement. One small calorie equals 4.186 J, and one food calorie equals to 4,186 J. Given the above information, it requires only one step to show that 1 food calorie is equal to about 4 BTUs: 4,186 J/cal/1,055 J/BTU = 3.97 BTUs/cal. In other words, a slice of bread with 80 calories can be expressed as approximately 318 BTUs (80 × 3.97 = 317.6) or 334,880 J (4186 × 80 = 334880 J).

By using one standard reference, the Joule, we see more clearly that energy merely takes different forms while performing various tasks. The same energy units that measure the dynamics of a locomotive can be used to analyze the metabolic rate of a living being.

Calculating the Tax on Gasoline and Home Energy Fuel

Returning to the original problem, we first compute the added cost of operating an automobile. *The Universal Almanac* tells us that, "An engine burning 8 gallons of gasoline releases 1 million (10^6) BTU."[11] Since the proposed tax on gasoline is 59.9¢ per 10^6 BTUs, it means an increase of 59.9¢ for each 8 gallons of gasoline purchased. If a car is driven an average of 12,000 miles a year and the average gas mileage is 20 miles per gallon, then 600 gallons must be purchased each year $(12 \times 10^3)/(2 \times 10^1) = 600$). Each 8 gallons of the 600 represents another 59.9¢. Since there are seventy-five 59.9 units in 600 gallons (600/8 = 75), the tax per year amounts to 75×59.9¢ = $44.93 = $45. (Recall we are using two significant figures.)

A more revealing number would be the actual increase in cost per gallon of gasoline. Since the increased cost on each gallon is not dependent on the number of miles driven nor the gas mileage received; it therefore gives a more universal expression of the tax increase, one that is more easily understood than the tax on BTUs. The figures above permit two very quick ways of calculating the added tax per gallon.

Very simply, since 8 gallons correspond to one million BTUs, dividing 59.9¢ by 8 gallons gives 7.5¢ per gallon extra. Alternatively, we can divide the increased cost per year ($44.93) by the number of gallons purchased in a year (600). This also yields 7.5¢ per gallon to two significant figures. So if you're presently paying $1.00 per gallon for gasoline, expect to be paying about $1.08 if this tax is enacted.

Next, a calculation for home fuel costs must be done with respect to both natural gas and heating oil. According to The Universal Almanac, the average BTU consumption per household in 1987 was 100 million BTUs.[12] This includes all energy use—space heating, appliances, air conditioning, and water heating. Three calculations: only gas consumption, only oil consumption, and an average of both, will give reasonable figures for the added tax burden on maintaining a home.

Recall that natural gas is to be taxed at 25.7¢ /10⁶ BTUs, and that heating oil is to be be taxed the same as gasoline at 59.9¢/10⁶ BTUs.

Case 1: If a household relies only on natural gas the added tax will be:

25.7¢/10^6 BTUs $\times 100 \times 10^6$ BTUs = $25.70.

Case 2: If a household relies only on home heating oil the added tax will be: 59.9¢/10^6 BTUs × 100 × 10^6 BTUs = $59.90.
Case 3: If both natural gas and home heating oil are used equally the added tax for the average will be: ($25.7 + $59.9)/2 = $42.80.

The total cost to the consumer is the added cost of gasoline needed to fuel at least one automobile and the added cost of home heating fuel. (Recall that $44.93 was the additional cost for maintaining one automobile.) The total costs are given for each of the three cases below:

1. $44.93 + $25.70 = $70.63 ($71 to the nearest dollar)
2. $44.93 + $59.90 = $104.83 ($100 assuming two significant figures)
3. $44.93 + $42.80 = $87.73 ($88 to the nearest dollar)

Finding the Per Capita Tax

The BTU tax is all inclusive. Farmers and manufacturers alike depend on energy in one form or another. If their additional costs are passed on to consumers then each of us will pay a share of the tax based on the total energy consumption for the United States. This is a worst case scenario for the consumer.

In 1988, the U.S. consumed 80,000 trillion BTUs (80 quadrillion BTUs or 80 × 10^{15}).[13] Using a population of 250 × 10^6, the per capita BTU consumption is: (80 × 10^{15} BTUs)/(25 × 10^6) = 320 × 10^6 BTUs/person. Approximately 42 percent of the energy used in the U.S. in 1988 was petroleum based.[14] Therefore: 42% of the 320 × 10^6 BTUs will be evaluated at 59.9¢ and the remaining 58% will be evaluated at 25.7¢ .

Calculation for Petroleum use at 42 percent:

.42 × 320 × 10^6 BTUs = 134.4 × 10^6 BTUs,
134.4 × 10^6 BTUs × 59.9¢/10^6 BTUs = $80.5

Calculation for all other energy use at 58 percent:

.58 × 320 × 10^6 BTUs = 185.6 × 10^6 BTUs,
185.6 × 10^6 BTUs × 25.7¢ /10^6 BTUs = $47.7

Total cost for both forms of energy:

$80.5 + $47.7 = $128.2 = $130 to two significant figures.

Therefore, the highest average tax for each consumer should not exceed $130 in the worst case. Of course, if you live in a large house, drive in excess of 12,000 miles a year, and make many and large purchases, your "worst case tax scenario" will be greater.

There is a large difference between per capita BTU use and per capita end-use. The difference between the two amounts is a measure of the waste inherent in the system. No process in nature is 100 percent efficient. It turned out that only 244 × 10^6 BTUs/person (end-use) of the 320 × 10^6 BTUs/person produced in 1988 was actually usable. The rest was lost in the generation, transmission, and distribution processes, where energy losses result from the creation of unwanted heat.

Fortunately for us, our utility bill reflects only our usage, we are not charged for transmission or distribution losses. However, we do pay for the energy losses (in the form of heat) from our appliances and autos. There is a lesson to be learned here. The more efficient our "end-use" of energy, the less of it is consumed and more money is saved. This makes fuel efficiency and conservation major players in saving money.

Looking a Little Deeper

Figure 6.1 shows car fuel efficiency standards for each year during the interval 1978-1991.[15] A simple average for this thirteen year period is 24.5 miles per gallon. But the average should really be "weighted" since the number of cars is not evenly distributed each year. This fact, in addition to the toll that wear and tear have on gas mileage, and the fact that fuel efficiency is measured under optimum conditions, is the reason 20 miles per gallon was chosen. See Figure 6.1 below. It should also be noted that Figure 6.1 pertains only to U.S. made automobiles. The contribution from imported cars slightly increases fuel efficiency each year. The weighted average U.S. fuel efficiency for passenger cars (assuming 55% city driving and 45% highway driving) as of 1988 was 19.17 miles per gallon.[16] If we factor in the slight increase in mileage due to imported vehicles, 20 miles per gallon is a reasonable estimate.

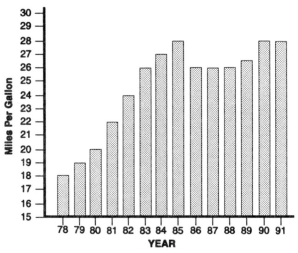

Figure 6.1
Graph showing U.S. car fuel standards

Source: Adapted from, *Environmental Almanic*, compiled by
World Resources Institute.

Had higher fuel efficiency standards been set during previous years, how much money could have been saved in 1991? Let's assume that higher standards would have boosted the present 20 miles per gallon to 24 miles per gallon and calculate the savings. In 1990, America had 145 million passenger cars. The average increase from 1985 to 1990 was approximately two million cars per year. Using this to extrapolate to 1991, gives an estimated 147 million automobiles.[17]

Since 24 miles per gallon reduces gas consumption to $5/6$ of what it is at 20 miles per gallon ($20/24 = 5/6$), each car consumes only 500 gallons per year ($5/6 \times 600 = 500$). (Recall that at 20 miles per gallon fuel consumption for an automobile driven 12,000 miles per year is 600 gallons.) If each car uses 100 gallons less fuel every year, at an average cost of $1.00 per gallon, this is a savings of $100.00 per auto. This works out to 147×10^6 cars $\times$ $100/car = 14.7×10^9, or $14,700,000,000.

Furthermore, if we perform a similar calculation (with the same assumptions) based on the per capita use for **all transportation**, the final figure would come to about $28 billion in savings. This number was calculated as follows: 42% of the fuel used in America is in the form of petroleum and about 62% of this is for transportation of all kinds.[18] If the per capita fuel consumption is 320×10^6 BTUs/person, then the amount of energy used by each American for transportation is:

320×10^6 BTUs/person $\times .42 \times .62 = 83.3 \times 10^6$ BTUs/person. Since 10^6 BTUs are equivalent to 8 gallons of gasoline, then $83.3 \times 8 = 666.4$ gallons are used for transportation, on average, for each person per year. If only $5/6$ the amount of gasoline is used, then each person consumes only 555.3 gallons of gas ($666.4 \times 5/6 = 555.3$ gal), thus saving on the cost of 111.1 gallons. The present population is 2.5×10^8, so at $1.00 per gallon, the savings equals $111.1 \times 2.5 \times 10^8 = 277.8×10^8, = 27.8×10^9 or about $28 billion. One can think of this number as a rough estimate of what the maximum savings for the American public in 1991 could have been with a modest gain in fuel efficiency over the years. Such an increase in fuel efficiency is by no means unreasonable today. "Indeed, one study covered in the UCS (Union of Concerned Scientists) book, *Steering a New Course*, concluded that fuel economy could cost-effectively be increased to over 40 mpg without sacrificing size or acceleration."[19] Additionally, the UCS and other environmental organizations believe "...there is tremendous opportunity for further efficiency gains without any sacrifice in safety."[20] Auto manufacturers usually cite decreased consumer safety as an argument against greater fuel efficiency standards.

Though Americans may have to endure higher energy taxes in order to bring down the deficit, there is no reason creative steps cannot be taken to alleviate some of this burden. Increasing fuel efficiency standards may dramatically help (over a period of years) balance out the cost of additional energy taxes. In the end, Americans will have more money in their pockets, which makes for a healthier economy. Before leaving Problem #3 do the exercises below:

> 1. Estimate the revenue the government can expect to raise from private energy use, assume two cars per household and one hundred million households.

Answer: Over $13 billion

> 2.a) Estimate the revenue again, but this time use the per capita information based on 320×10^6 BTUs/person, assuming equal shares of petroleum and all other energy sources.
> b) Recalculate part (a) using petroleum as the only energy source.

Answers: a) $32 billion   b) $50 billion

The above two problems make it clear that figures read in newspapers and quoted by analysts can easily be misunderstood unless the initial conditions are emphasized. How would these numbers change if the above calculations were done based on the end-use per capita figure?

> 3. It is interesting to note that the U.S. produced only 67 quadrillion BTUs in 1988;[21] find the percentage of energy the U.S. imported for this year.

Answer 16%

There is much more that can be said about all three of the problems we have discussed. Each one has a complex mixture of social, political, and mathematical components. When problems are placed within the perspective of history, culture, and science, we can see more clearly that there are few truly simple problems. Only by understanding all of the different attributes of a problem can lasting and positive solutions be found.

The nineties hold great promise for personal health, efficient resource use, and improving our economy. But we must understand those factors that influence our personal and political choices, and appreciate the insight science and mathematics can contribute to our decisions.

CHAPTER SEVEN

Beyond Arithmetic

Arithmetical operations are immensely useful but can be taken only so far. We have reached a point where geometry and algebra need to be applied to the concepts of the previous chapters. Hopefully, the reader will see that without these concepts, exploring more involved real-world problems is not possible.

Explanations and definitions are given as the need arises. Though the reader is assumed to know little of the subject, he or she is required to remember well what has been stated. It may be best to have a pencil handy when reading the next two chapters and to proceed slowly. Much can still be gained by reading Chapters Seven and Eight even if all the mathematics is not initially understood.

*   *   *

Since we relate better to pictures than words or numbers, mathematical equations are usually represented graphically. When it comes to science, the expression, "One picture is worth a thousand words" is invaluable, especially when that "picture" is in the form of a graph. Interestingly enough, the idea of using mathematical relationships to describe reality goes back to antiquity, but the notion of associating a formula with a graph to express real-world phenomena is relatively recent. We begin an exploration of these ideas and their uses by treading back a few hundred years.

*   *   *

It wasn't until the sixteenth century that the idea of a stationary Earth and geocentric model (Earth centered) of the universe began to crumble. Copernicus's book *De Revolutions*, which advocated a heliocentric (sun centered) solar system, was published at the time of his death. Many believe this was intended to protect Copernicus from difficulties with the Church, which dogmatically held to a geocentric view. For Copernicus, the attraction of a heliocentric model of the solar system was its geometric and mathematical simplicity. This attitude, reducing complex ideas to the simplest possible mathematical and geometrical representations, is at the heart of modern scientific thought.

The structure of the geocentric universe in the sixteenth century was based largely on the writings of Ptolemy, and before him, Aristotle. It was a complicated mixture of circular motions like those inside a spring-wound watch. The need for such complexity arose by insisting that the Earth occupy the center of creation and that all heavenly motion be circular. The reasoning behind this unyielding paradigm (the geocentric concept was accepted for 1800 years) was based on erroneous perception and inflated ego. It **appeared** that all creation circled about the Earth and that God's grandest creation, man, should occupy center stage. It was also terribly difficult to argue for a moving Earth, since "common sense" told people they were not in motion. But Copernicus favored mathematical simplicity over appearance and dogma. Since his heliocentric model gave similar results to the geocentric model, why bother, he reasoned, to keep the more complicated structure. Copernicus's belief in the economy of creation is still echoed today.

Though Copernicus's model was closer to reality than Ptolemy's, it was still seriously flawed. Copernicus had correctly reasoned that the sun was the central body of the solar system but he held to the classical Greek view that the circle, "being the most perfect of forms," must necessarily represent the orbits of all heavenly bodies.

By the year 1600, the Danish astronomer Tycho Brahe (1546-1601) had compiled the most accurate planetary data then known.

Tycho, though an extraordinary astronomer, lacked the mathematical savvy necessary to refine Copernicus's planetary model. But Tycho's assistant, Johannes Kepler, who inherited the data after Tycho's death, did possess the mathematical sophistication and perseverance to properly analyze it. After two decades of work, Kepler had finished the last of what has become known as Kepler's Three Laws of Planetary Motion.

Kepler's first law transformed Copernicus's circular orbits into ellipses which produced a more accurate model for planetary motion. His other two laws involved the changing velocities planets undergo in their motion about the sun and the relationship between a planet's periodicity and its distance from the sun.

The significance of both Copernicus's and Kepler's work was in the preeminent role mathematics played in describing the physical world. They had transcended classical Greek thought by allowing the data to freely determine the geometry, rather than a supposed geometry forcing itself upon the "data." To the Greeks, "data" was meaningless, since they did not usually conduct experiments. Their "data" involved observing nature and then forming conclusions without testing. Curiously, modern physicists are more apt to place geometry (symmetries in nature) above all else. Perhaps we have come full circle.

Galileo Galilei was a contemporary of Kepler. He, more than anyone, is often credited with being the first true experimental scientist. Galileo conducted well designed experiments, wherein data was collected and analyzed mathematically. He sought relationships between variables, such as time and distance. One of Galilieo's many achievements was discovering the relationship between time and distance for falling objects near the Earth's surface. Much of his data analysis and thought experiments disproved a good deal of classical Greek thinking.

You may remember from your school days that it was Galileo who presumably dropped two different weights from the Tower of Pisa and showed that both reached the ground in essentially the same time—thereby proving all objects fall at the same rate. What you may not remember, is that his discovery showed that the mathematical relationship between time and distance for a falling object is nonlinear. That is to say, a falling object (strictly speaking in a vacuum) does not fall equal distances in equal intervals of time. Just as Copernicus and Kepler had done, Galileo let the data interpret the physical world. In the second half of the seventeenth century, the famous Sir Isaac Newton unified the work of Kepler and Galileo into three basic laws of nature which accurately described terrestrial and heavenly motion.

*   *   *

The key idea in using mathematical data is in defining the correct relationship between the **independent** variable and the **dependent** variable. For instance, if a person is paid five dollars an hour for performing a task, then his earnings are **dependent** on the time he works. **Time is therefore the independent variable, and earnings, the dependent variable.** A simple formula can be written for this relationship. If "t" represents the time worked, then $5.00 × t equals the money earned. The only algebra involved is in replacing the variable "t" with the appropriate number of hours worked. For example, if 4 hours and 45 minutes (4.75 hours) are worked, the pay is $5.00/hour × 4.75 hours = $23.75.

Often, when dealing with algebraic formulas, the multiplication symbol × is not written. This is done to eliminate any confusion between the multiplication symbol × and the variable x, thus simplifying the notation. The expression $5.00 × t, is therefore written as $5.00t, where the multiplication is now implicitly understood.

During the sixteenth and seventeenth centuries, there was much debate between the primacy of algebra over geometry or vice versa.[1] The philosopher-mathematician Rene Descartes (1596-1650) is usually credited with merging the two fields together into analytic geometry, or as it is also called, coordinate geometry. Descartes, however, never actually made use of any coordinate system. His contribution was in providing the idea for associating algebraic formulas with geometrical shapes. Those who followed him were responsible for the creation of what has become known as the Cartesian Coordinate System.[2]

The Cartesian Coordinate System

The Cartesian coordinate system is a useful tool for understanding many present day problems. An explanation of the Cartesian coordinate system begins with the number line.

The typical number line has zero placed at its center with negative numbers to the left and positive numbers to the right. The number line in Figure 7.1 is one-dimensional, meaning only one variable is used to describe a quantity. A thermometer is an example of a vertical

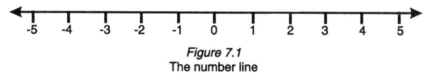

Figure 7.1
The number line

number line with temperature as the only variable.

Number lines offer a concise visual representation of numerical data. Figure 7.2 shows the distances between Santa Barbara,

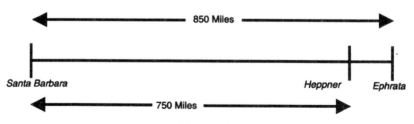

Figure 7.2
Using a number line as a visual aid

California and Heppner, Oregon, as well as between Santa Barbara and Ephrata, Washington. The lengths of the two lines gives an immediate "feel" of the comparative distances.

To investigate the relationship between two variables, two number lines, one for each variable, are needed. The lines, however, are arranged perpendicular to each other as in Figure 7.3. The negative parts of the number lines have been omitted for simplicity.

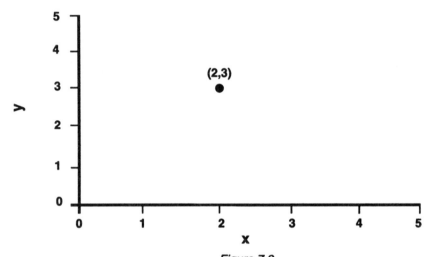

Figure 7.3
Two number lines at right angles forming
a two dimensional coordiante plane with the
ordered pair (2,3) plotted.

The two number lines form a coordinate plane, or a Cartesian Coordinate System. The horizontal number line is called the x-axis and the vertical number line is called the y-axis. To locate a position (a point) in the plane an "ordered pair" (or set of coordinates) is required. For example, in Figure 7.3 the ordered pair (2,3) represents the point in the plane that is located two units to the right of the point (0,0)—**called the origin**—and three units above the x-axis. **The horizontal distance from the origin is called the x-coordinate or abscissa, and the vertical distance from the x-axis is called the y-coordinate or ordinate.**

Had we wished to plot the point (3,2) rather than (2,3), we would have gone over 3 and up 2. The first coordinate in the parentheses, 2, in the first example we chose, is associated with the horizontal direction or x-axis. Similarly, the second coordinate, 3, is associated with the vertical direction or y-axis. This is why the term "ordered pair" is used.

Ordered pairs can be generated by using a formula or by collecting data. More often than not, real-world problems are investigated by collecting data and then plotting points (ordered pairs) in the coordinate plane to generate a "scatter plot." Hopefully, a pattern emerges between the two variables that can be interpreted and extrapolated. The statistician, business person, and social and physical scientist, all try to find a "mathematical model" (an equation) that describes the relationship between the two variables. Once the correct relationship is found (that is, an equation is determined) the art of prediction making can be taken seriously. For instance, a graph that shows a correlation between the number of breast cancer deaths and fat consumption can be used to predict the optimum daily fat consumption, and the risks associated with varying levels of fat intake.

Classroom instruction in mathematics does not focus on data collection. The student is usually subjected to endless formulas without any real-world meaning. Only those few students who take courses in chemistry and physics begin to see how the mathematics they have studied is actually applied. Otherwise, students spend their time plugging the x-value into a given formula, which in turn produces a y-value, thereby obtaining ordered pairs which are then plotted on graph paper. This type of procedure always yields perfect looking relationships between variables, which is not the case in the real world. Even my gifted students were confounded when presented with real-world data for the first time. In a sense, they have been brainwashed; they do not see that in the real world most formulas represent tendencies, and not exact relationships. Students spend so much time seeing perfect curves emerge with formulas that they fail to see that nature, at best, only approximates these ideal shapes. Most students are not provided with an opportunity to plot real data for the purpose of **discovering** relationships.

Formulas and Data

An example of using a formula to generate ordered pairs can be shown with the algebraic expression $5.00t cited earlier.

Recall that "t" represented the time worked and the product $5.00t represented the money earned. In equation form, this is written as:

money earned = $5.00t, or as, y = $5.00t where y stands for the earnings and t represents time in hours and plays the role of x. It doesn't matter if we call the x-axis the t-axis as long as it's the horizontal axis.

To generate ordered pairs from this formula, we insert t values and compute the corresponding y values (e.g., if t = 5, y = $25).

Table 7.1

Values generated using the equation y = $5.00t

Time(t)	Earnings(y)
0	0
1	$ 5.00
2	$10.00
3	$15.00
4	$20.00
5	$25.00
6	$30.00
7	$35.00
8	$40.00

The values in Table 7.1 can be expressed as the ordered pairs: (0,0), (1,$5.00), (2,$10.00), (3,$15.00), (4,$20.00) (5,$25.00), (6,$30.00), (7,$35.00), (8,$40.00). These points are graphed in Figure 7.4.

Notice how perfectly straight the points line up—a result of plugging numbers into a formula. A straight line is drawn through the points in Figure 7.4, thus allowing one to read off earnings for other than the whole number of hours worked. No data collection was needed to generate this graph. The equation was determined by the pay rate, which was given. Now let's consider a real-world problem.

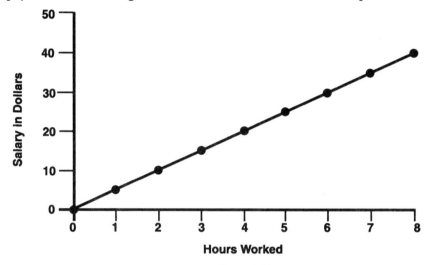

Figure 7.4
Graph showing money earned at a rate of $5.00 per hour

Data was collected from various countries for a 1975 study using fat consumption in grams per day and the number of breast cancer deaths per 100,000 females (Table 7.2).

Table 7.2

Fat Consumption and Breast Cancer Deaths

Country	Fat Consumption Grams/Day	Deaths/100,000
Thailand	24.9	0.75
Japan	35.3	3.56
El Salvador	39.7	1.13
Taiwan	42.4	4.43
Ceylon	46.0	2.44

Country	Fat Consumption Grams/Day	Deaths/100,000
Panama	56.5	7.44
Bulgaria	66.6	8.33
Portugal	67.2	12.74
Yugoslavia	70.8	6.43
Poland	86.6	10.59
Czechoslovakia	90.8	14.64
Hungary	96.5	13.21
Austria	116.8	16.54
Australia	128.4	18.57
Germany	134.4	16.67
Switzerland	135.0	21.36
Canada	140.1	23.18
United States	146.0	20.45
Netherlands	152.6	26.00

Source: Carroll,K., "Experimental Evidence of Dietary Factors in Hormone Dependent Cancers" Cancer Research, 35:3374, 1975

Data interpolated from graph: error ±2.0 grams/day, ±.20 deaths/100,000[3]

The second column—Fat Consumption in Grams/Day—provides the horizontal data and the third column—Deaths/100,000—provides the vertical data. An example of an ordered pair for this data set is (24.9,0.75) for Thailand. A scatter plot of Table 7.2 is given in Figure 7.5.

The first thing to look for in Figure 7.5 is a general trend. It appears that as fat consumption increases so does the number of deaths. This means there is a correlation between the two variables. But can the correlation be best represented with a straight line or a curved line? Since there is no obvious curvature to the data, a **linear-fit** (straight line) is the simplest and most reasonable approach.

The line in Figure 7.5 represents the general trend of the data. There are a number of different mathematical ways to determine

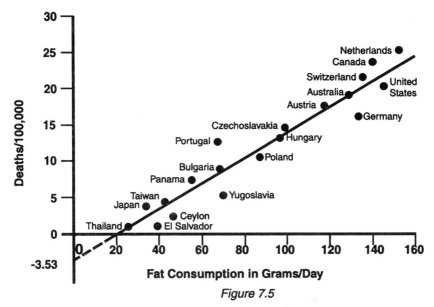

Figure 7.5

**A scatter plot showing breast cancer deaths per 100,000
females verses fat consumed per day**

Source: Adapted from a graph in John Robbin's
Diet for a New America. Original source:
Carroll, K., "Cancer Research," 35:3374, 1975

what is called a "**best-fit line**" for a scatter plot. None of these concerns us here. For our purposes it is enough to ask the reader to "**eyeball**" a line, i.e., sight along the data and draw a line that seems like a good representation of the trend.

Notice where the **trend-line** in figure 7.5 intersects the horizontal axis. The intersection is at approximately 20 grams of fat per day. This amount of fat represents about 10 percent of the calories [(20 × 9)/2000] × 100 = 9% on a 2000 calorie diet. Recall that the recommended percentage of calories derived from fat is 30 percent. Using the trend line we see that 67 grams of fat (which is equivalent to 30 percent fat consumption for a 2000 calorie diet) corresponds to about 8 deaths per 100,000—an improvement over the 1975 figure of 20 per 100,000 for the United States (see Figure 7.5 or Table 7.2).

Might we do better by reducing our fat consumption to 10 percent of our total caloric intake instead of the recommended 30 percent?

It is important to properly understand what a trend line means. The closer the data points cluster around the trend line the better the fit. In the ideal case, the line would go through every data point like the contrived salary example. The better the trend line is matched to the data, the greater the confidence we have in using the equation of the trend line to relate the two variables.

Scientifically, it is hoped that the equation used to describe the trend line represents the true relationship between the variables, admitting an accepted range of error. The more the data is scattered about the line in a random fashion without major deviations, the more apt we are to believe the fit is a true expression of reality. Then again, if the data were biased in one direction or if there was a distinctive curve away from the straight line fit, this would cause grave concern. Yet we might temporarily ignore such problems if the errors involved were not substantial. But under no condition would we believe such a trend line is the correct statement for relating the two variables. This brings up a somewhat philosophical point.

*   *   *

What made Kepler certain that the planets of our solar system travel in ellipses about the sun? He used Tycho's data for the planet Mars and found that the closest shape that fit the orbit was an ellipse. It should be pointed out that this conclusion was not at all obvious at the time, since the elliptical shape of Mars' orbit is nearly circular. But do the planets travel in perfect ellipses? Kepler's work shows (and Newton's universal theory of gravity confirms) that if only one force (due to the sun) acts on each planet, then each planet follows the path of a perfect ellipse. Only under this condition does the equation for an ellipse hold. But everything is connected. Some things are just connected more strongly than others.

The gravitational effects of the other planets of the solar system, and every star and particle of matter in the universe, are far too weak to perturb the overall elliptical motion of the planets as they orbit the sun. But regardless of how small these affects may be, they do still exist. In reality, the planets do not travel in orbits that repeat their motion over the same path. Their motion is therefore not exactly elliptical. We can easily account for the effects of the larger planets of the solar system, but not every particle of matter in the universe, nor is it necessary to do so. We ignore them because they will not influence our observations or calculations in any significant way. We can still predict where Mars will be at 10:00 P.M. on March 8, 2061. By assuming elliptical motion, we can send a spacecraft to orbit Mars or have Viking landers explore its surface. It matters little to the engineer if the geometric center of Mars is a fraction of an inch off of where the theoretical (elliptical) equation predicts.

From our vantage point, an ellipse expresses nature's structure for planetary orbits. But in reality, it is an incredibly good approximation—not truth. No equation **perfectly** describes any real-world phenomena. Ultimately, every equation that is written to explain a real-world situation is an idealized view of reality. So does mathematics describe objective reality or merely humankind's subjective "macroscopic" view? The best we can say is that the better the data fits our chosen mathematical model, the better we understand how the variables in question relate to each other. We do not lightly ignore other variables, but choose judiciously those that are considered to provide the best results and offer the greatest insights.

Finding the Equation of a Trend Line

It was shown previously that by plugging numbers into an equation, a series of points could be generated that formed a straight line. The reverse process is also possible; an equation can be determined from a line. Once a trend line is drawn, it represents the relationship between the variables in our experiment. Any process used to find the equation of a line can equally be applied to finding the equation of a trend line. This assumes we are merely taking our "best guess" at a representative line through the data—drawing it in by hand—rather than a mathematical approach.

Consider the trend line in figure 7.5, where Thailand appears to fall exactly on the line. If we had the equation for the trend line, we could insert the value for fat consumption (24.9 grams/day) and the equation would give the experimental value of .75 deaths/100,000. But if the fat consumption value for El Salvador (39.7 grams/day) were inserted, the equation would give a value closer to Japan's 3.56 deaths/100,000 rather than El Salvador's 1.13 deaths/100,000. One can, however, mathematically compute a reasonable error range for a scatter plot and its associated trend line. This is why it is not uncommon to see numbers such as 50.3 ± 2.5 arising from statistical results. Such numbers mean that there is a very high probability that if the experiment were performed, the answer would be some where between 47.8 and 52.8 for a given x value. It is unnecessary for our purposes to digress into the mechanics of error analysis. Just bear in mind that trend lines are not expected to yield exact answers, only reasonable approximations.

*   *   *

In the spirit of Descartes, we wish to find a relationship between an algebraic equation and a straight line. Odd as it may sound, right triangles are used to provide the needed insight.

A right triangle has two "legs" which meet at a 90° (right) angle and are referred to as the base and height of the triangle, and a third side connecting the two legs called the hypotenuse (see Figure 7.6). Any diagonal line can serve as the hypotenuse of an infinite number of right triangles.

In Figure 7.7 a line (ACE) is drawn in the coordinate plane with two triangles. The large triangle (ADE) and the small triangle (ABC) both share the line as their hypotenuse. The base AD has a length of 8 units and the height DE is 40 units. The ratio of the height to the

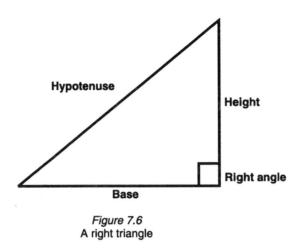

Figure 7.6
A right triangle

Figure 7.7
The ratio of height to base for any right triangle
constructed in a like manner will be the same.

base (height/base) is 40/8. The same ratio holds for the smaller triangle, where the height/base is 25/5. For that matter, any right triangle that is formed by adjoining vertical and horizontal lines to the hypotenuse will give the same ratio of height/base. This is no coincidence. **All straight lines have what is known as a constant slope, defined by the ratio of height/base.** Since the height is a measure of the y value and the base is a measure of the x value, we can express this ratio as y/x = 5. **This is true only if the line contains the point (0,0).** The relationship y/x = 5, is really the equation of the hypotenuse and can be rewritten as y = 5x. This is done by multiplying each side by x. A concrete example will help: 10/2 = 5, let the 10 play the role of y, and 2 play the role of x. If each side of the equation is multiplied by 2 we have: $10/2 \times 2 = 5 \times 2$. The left side equals 10 (or y) and the right side equals 5×2 (or 5x). As long as the equation balances, each side still equals the other, nothing incorrect has been done. Any mathematical process is valid if the same mathematical operation is performed on each side of an equation. See the end of this chapter for more examples of this.

The equation y = 5x is identical to y = \$5.00t (x and t represent unknowns), and therefore has the same graph. Since any straight line can have a horizontal and a vertical line adjoined to it, thus making a right triangle, the equation of the line can be found. **If the line contains the point (0,0) then the equation of the line can be found by finding the slope (height/base) of the line.** For example, if the ratio height/base for a line is 7, then y/x = 7; multiplying both sides by x gives y = 7x as the equation of the line.

The slope of a line is also referred to as the "**rise over the run**" as well as the ratio of height/base. If the line were nearly vertical then the triangle would have a small base (run) and large height (rise), meaning the slope is a large number. By the same reasoning, if the base (run) were large and the height (rise) small, the line would be closer to horizontal and its slope would be a small number. The ratio of the rise (height) to the run (base) is an indication of how the line is oriented in the coordinate plane. How would the line be oriented in the plane if the rise and run were equal? If the height were zero and the base any number?

When t = 0 (no time worked) in the equation y = \$5.00t, the wage y is also 0. The graph of the line y = \$5.00t, therefore passes through the center of the coordinate system (0,0), **the origin**. Unfortunately, if a line does not go through the origin we cannot find its slope and consequently its equation by forming the simple ratio y/x as we did previously. To find the slope, and therefore the equation of any line in the plane, requires one additional step.

Finding the General Equation of a Line

To investigate the equation of a line not constrained to pass through the origin, we use the following example.

Many repair people charge an hourly rate and an additional fee for making a house call. Let's say a T.V. repair person charges a set fee of $35.00 just to walk through your door, and an hourly fee of $20.00. Therefore, at t = 0 you already owe $35.00. After the first hour of work, you owe $35.00 + $20.00/hour × 1 hour, after the second hour, $35.00 + $20.00/hour × 2 hours and so on. The general equa-

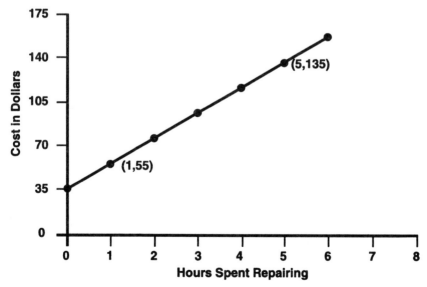

Figure 7.8
Graph showing cost to repair a T.V. over a six hour period

tion that represents this is: Cost = \$35.00 + \$20.00t or c = \$35.00 + \$20.00t. It is understood that c (the cost) is playing the role of y, and t (the time) means the same as x.

Several ordered pairs for this equation are:

(0 hours, \$35.00), (1 hour, \$55.00), (2 hours, \$75.00).

Figure 7.8 is a graph of the equation c = \$35.00 + \$20.00t. Notice that it is offset from the origin, and is oriented differently than the line y = \$5.00t.

Do the ratios of c/t formed in Figure 7.8 yield constant values? For example, does \$55.00/1 = \$75.00/2? No. But (\$55.00 − \$35.00)/1 equals (\$75.00 − \$35.00)/2. Subtracting \$35.00 removes the offset, and therefore preserves the rule for y/x.*

Any two points (x_1, y_1) and (x_2, y_2), where the subscripts, 1 and 2, stand for the first and second points picked, can be used to find a rise and a run. When the two y's are subtracted from each other $(y_2 − y_1)$ the offset is canceled out. For instance, using the two points (1,55) and (5,135) gives \$135 − \$55 = \$80 for the rise. By expressing \$55.00 as \$35.00 + \$20.00, and \$135 as \$35.00 + \$100.00, it is easier to see how the \$35.00 cancels out. The calculation is: (\$35.00 + \$100.00) − (\$35.00 + \$20.00) = **\$35.00 − \$35.00** + (\$100 − \$20) = \$80.00.

The general expression for the slope is: $(y_2 − y_1)/(x_2 − x_1)$

and the general equation for a line can be written as:

y = mx + b, where the m represents the slope, and **b** the offset, commonly called the **y-intercept** (that is, where the line intersects the y axis).

We can now verify that c = \$35 + \$20t (or c = 20t + 35, using the form y = mx + b) is the equation for the repair work.

The slope can be found using any two points on the line. For example, using the points (1,55) and (5,135) yields: m = (135 −

* Whenever a slope is stated as y/x there is an implied understanding that y/x is really (y-0)/(x-0). The differences in the y-values and x-values are often referred to as "delta-y" and "delta-x" values, written as Δy and Δx.

55)/(5 − 1) = 80/4 = $20.00/h.

Similarly, for the points (2,75) and (4,115) we have:
m = (115 − 75)/(4 − 2) = 40/2 = $20.00/h.

We already know that $35.00 is equal to b, since it is the offset. Hence, y = mx + b is c = ($20.00/h)t + $35.00, where the roles of (x,y) are played by (t,c).

We are now in a position to determine the equation of the trend line in Figure 7.5. Ignoring the data, we choose any two points that we can accurately read on the line. (Remember, a line is composed of an infinite number of points.) Fortuitously, there are a number of data points that lie on the line, so determining the correct coordinates will be easy. It is usually best to choose two points that span as much of the data set as possible; for our case this means choosing Thailand (24.9,.75) and Australia (128.4,18.57).

The slope m equals: (18.57 − .75)/(128.4 − 24.9), and reduces to approximately .172 deaths per one hundred thousand women, per gram of fat consumed per day. Since we do not know "b" yet, all we can write is, y = .172x + b.

The unknown "b" can be found by extending the line and reading off where it crosses the y-axis, or mathematically by inserting any ordered pair (x,y) on the line into the equation y = .172x + b.

To better understand this last statement, consider the numerically simpler example: y = 2x + b and the point (3,12) known to be on the line. By plugging in for x and y we have: 12 = 2(3) + b. The unknown b can be found by subtracting 2(3) from each side of the equation [12 − 2(3) = 2(3) − 2(3) + b]. Recall that any operations are permissible as long as the same operation is performed on each side of the equation. This leaves 6 = b or b = 6, since the unknown is commonly written on the left. The final equation in our simplified example is: y = 2x + 6.

Returning to the original problem (y = .172x + b), it is already known that both (24.9,.75) and (128.4,18.57) are on the line, so either point can be used to find b. Since it does not matter which point we choose, we'll select the first point, (24.9,.75). Therefore: .75

= .172(24.9) + b, subtracting .172(24.9) from each side of the equation yields, b = −3.53. Now that m and b are known, the equation of the trend line can be written as: y = .172x − 3.53.

The above equation is the mathematical model relating breast cancer deaths to fat consumption. The model predicts that if 180 grams of fat are eaten per day, the incidence of breast cancer will be: y = .172(180) − 3.53, or 27.4 deaths/100,000. (Where we use only three significant figures.) It would be surprising if this answer were correct, because of the scatter of the real data about our model. Therefore, the y value should be stated with a plus or minus (±) range of values as previously discussed. Though it is not an accepted method for error analysis, finding the maximum difference between the model's value and the experimental value, for a given x, can give an upper bound on the error range. Remember, even with proper error analysis, predicted values represent only one possible answer out of a narrow range of possibilities.

As stated previously, the line crosses the x-axis at about 20 grams of fat, which means that the model predicts that close to 20 grams of fat consumption per day (remember there is error) is optimum for reducing breast cancer deaths. But what does the y-intercept, −3.53, tell us?

The y-intercept has no meaning here. It says that if zero fat is eaten there will be −3.53 deaths per hundred thousand females. Such "information" is meaningless, especially since without fat in our diets we would die. Like so many things, too little or too much can be hazardous.

For values less than 20 grams of fat, the mathematical model (y = .172x − 3.53) "breaks down" and is of no use. It is also unreasonable to assume that the model remains linear (straight) for ever increasing values of fat consumption. Students often memorize formulas pertaining to the real world, thinking them universal statements. Such formulas do not exist. All mathematical models (equations) have a limited domain over which they can yield meaningful results. A proper understanding of any physical process is necessary before attempting to extrapolate and predict with a model.

The slope of the line also provides information. In the first example, a slope of $5.00/hour indicated the rate of pay was constant. In the breast cancer example, the slope of .172 gives the number of women per 100,000 dying for each gram of fat eaten over 20 grams per day.

On a graph with the y-axis representing distance traveled and the x-axis representing time, the slope has units of distance over time which is defined as speed. The slope of real-world data is a meaningful ratio. Most basic algebra books ignore this fact, and instead focus on the ratio of dimensionless quantities. (Dimensionless in this context means there are no units assigned to the numbers—no hours, miles, grams, etc.. Most dimensionless problems have no connection to the real world.) Even when units are given, mathematics text books and mathematics teachers are not prone to emphasize their importance.

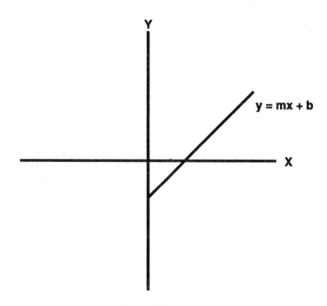

Figure 7.9a
A single-valued function

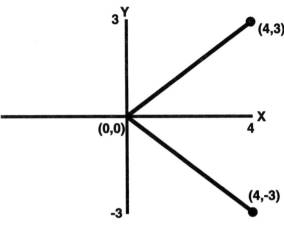

Figure 7.9b

An example of a graph that is not a function.
The points (4,3) and (4,-3) are just two of an
infinite number of points that disqualify the
graph as a function.

Functions

A function is a special kind of relationship. Specifically, it is a unique relationship between the independent variable (the x-coordinate) and the dependent variable (the y-coordinate), where each independent variable must be associated with only one dependent variable. In the salary example, the worker is never paid two different sums for the same time worked; $y = \$5.00t$ is therefore a function. Any equation that represents a straight line (all equations with the form $y = mx + b$) is a function—more correctly, a linear function. Study Figures 7.9a and 7.9b; the first is a function, the second one isn't.

In Figure 7.9a each ordered pair has a different x associated with a different y; it is thus a function—in particular, a **single-valued function**. Figure 7.9b, however, has two different y values for each x value, with the exception of (0,0); this disqualifies it from being a function. **Specifically, if a vertical line intersects the graph in more than one place, the graph does not represent a functional relationship.** Furthermore, **if a horizontal line intersects the graph only once, the graph is a single-valued function.** And if a horizontal line intersects the graph in more than one place, it is a multi-valued function. Often if the line intersects in just two places, the function is referred to as double-valued.

Figure 7.10 is an example of a multi-valued function. It shows how

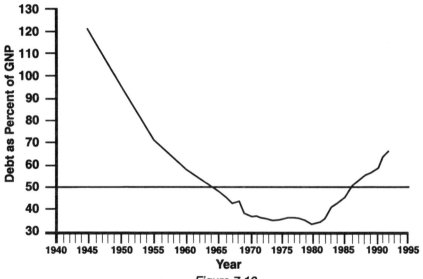

Figure 7.10

The percentage of GNP to national debt can be
viewed as a multi-valued function.
Source: *Abstract of the United States 1992,*
          U.S. Department of Commerce, Bureau of the Census

the percentage of national debt to GNP has changed over time.

A horizontal line drawn across the graph at the 50 percent level intersects at two different corresponding times (1964 and 1986). Other horizontal lines (below the 50% level) have more than two different x values for the same y value, hence the more proper designation as **multi**-valued. (A certain liberty is being taken with this example, since the 50 percent mark does not correspond exactly to 1964 and 1986.)

Figure 7.10 is a double-valued function when y equals 50 percent because two different independent variables are paired with the same dependent variable—(1964,50%) and (1986,50%). If the situation were reversed (that is, if the x values were the same and the y values were different, e.g., (1964,50%) and (1964,65%) then Figure 7.10 would not represent a function; nor would it make any sense within the given context.

Much of the physical world can be described with functions, which is why the study of mathematics takes on such importance. Everything from biological growth to the motion of the Earth through space can be written as a mathematical function.

Below are several exercises to help reinforce some of the concepts covered in this chapter. It is important that you at least read over problem 2, since we return to it in the next chapter.

Exercises

Find the value of "b" for the following problems.
1. $y = 3x + b$, (3,15) is on the given line.   Answer: $b = 6$.
2. $y = 2x + b$, (6,8) is on the given line.   Answer: $b = -4$.
3. $2y = 3.5x + b$, (0,2) is on the given line.   Answer: $b = 4$.
4. $y/2 = x + b$, (6,12) is on the given line.   Answer: $b = 0$.

(A similar problem to the ones above was worked out on Page 139)

Problems:

There are four problems given below. Problems 1 and 2 are worked out, Problems 3 and 4 are not. Study Problems 1 and 2 and then do Problems 3 and 4 on your own.

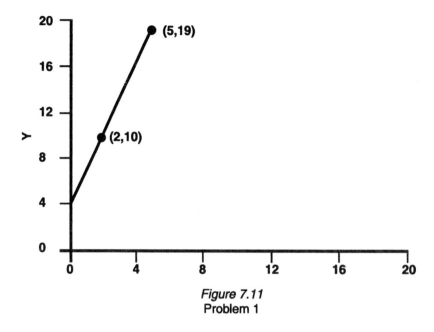

Figure 7.11
Problem 1

1. Two points determine a line. Given the points (2,10) and (5,19) determine the equation of the line that passes through them.

The objective is to find an equation with the form y = mx + b, where m and b are the unknown constants to be found.

First plot the two points and then draw the line they form (see Figure 7.11). It is not really necessary to draw the line, but a visual aid is always helpful.

The ratio of the height to the base for a right triangle constructed on this line equals the slope of the line m. The difference between the two given y values is (19 − 10). Similarly, the difference between the two given x values is (5 − 2). Therefore, the slope is m = (19 − 10)/(5 − 2) = 3. Knowing the slope allows us to write: y = 3x + b. Since the graph intersects the y-axis at 4, this must be b.

Often the intercept is found mathematically, because it cannot always be read off the graph so simply. This is done by replacing the x and y (in y = 3x + b) with any coordinates that are on the line. Since

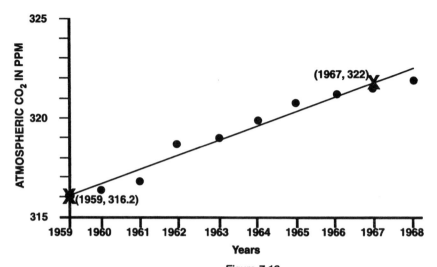

Figure 7.12

CO_2 in parts per million from 1959-1968.

Source: Adapted from, *Vital Signs 1992*,
Worldwatch Institute

both (2,10) and (5,19) are on the line, either one can be substituted. Choosing (2,10) yields: 10 = 3(2) + b, or 10 = 6 + b. Subtracting 6 from each side of the equation gives, b = 4. Having found m = 3 and b = 4, the equation of the line can now properly be written as, y = 3x + 4.

Any value of x the reader chooses for the equation y = 3x + 4 will produce a corresponding value of y such that the ordered pair (x,y) must be on the line in Figure 7.11. Try inserting 5 for x to convince yourself that (5,19) is indeed on the line.

> 2. Figure 7.12 is a scatter plot of the atmospheric concentration of carbon dioxide in ppm from 1959 to 1968. The data is given as (year,ppm): (1959,316.2), (1960,316.7), (1961,317.2), (1962,318.9), (1963,319.2), (1964,320), (1965,320.9), (1966,321.5), (1967,321.8), (1968,322.5).
> a) Assuming this data to be linear, "eye-ball" a best-fit line and determine its equation.

b) Predict the concentration of carbon dioxide in the year 2000, for this model. (We will discuss this problem more thoroughly in Chapter Eight.)

c) How reliable is the answer for part b?

Answers

a) The line passes through the data point (1959,316.2) and through the point (1967,322), which is not a data point. The slope of the line is: m = (322 − 316.2)/(1967 − 1959), which gives .725 ppm/year. Thus, so far we have: $y = .725x + b$. To find b, the temptation is to use 316.2 since this is where the line intersects the y-axis. However, **the y-intercept b is defined where x is zero**. Since we do not know the y-value when x equals zero (it is far off the graph), we must plug in one of the given points and solve for b. Using the first point (1959,316.2) gives:

$$316.2 = .725(1959) + b, \quad b = 316.2 − .725(1959) \text{ or } −1104.$$

The equation linking the variables of time and atmospheric carbon dioxide can then be written as: $y = .725x − 1104$.

There is an option that we could have used to simplify the numbers in this problem. It is perfectly correct to define 1959 as the zero year, and express the x-axis from 0 to 10. The equation would then simply be: $y = .725x + 316.2$

For instance, if we wish to calculate the ppm value in 1949 with this model, the first equation gives:

$y = .725(1949) − 1104$ which works out to 309 ppm. Using the second equation, we insert −10 for 1949, since 1959 = 0, thus giving us: $y = .725(−10) + 316.2$ which also works out to 309 ppm.

b) If "year 0" corresponds to 1959 then "year 41" corresponds to 2000. Using the second equation above we get:

$y = .725(41) + 316.2$ which gives 345.9 ppm.

c) The year 2000 is quite far beyond our last data point in 1968, so caution needs to be exercised here—unless we are sure that the rate of increase remains constant for the rest of the century. Had the question read 1975 instead of 2000, there would be less cause for concern, since we would not have to extrapolate so far into the "future." We will look more deeply into the implication of a limited data set (as in this problem) in the next chapter.

3. Find the equation of the line given the points (3,17) and (6,29). Don't forget to draw the line as a visual aid.

Answer: $y = 4x + 5$

4. Table 7.3 is a summary of the results of a study done across various countries in an attempt to find an association between the amount of cow's milk consumed in liters per year and the annual incidence of diabetes for children of ages 0 to 14.

Table 7.3

Table showing milk consumption rate for various countries and the corresponding incidence of childhood diabetes for children ages of 0-14.

Country	Liters Consumed Annually	Diabetes/100,000
Japan	38	1.4
France	79	4.4
Israel	90	3.9
Canada	107	8.9
United States	107	13.3
Netherlands	114	9.5
Great Britain	134	14.7
New Zealand	138	11.4
Denmark	138	13.7
Sweden	169	22.8
Norway	183	20.0
Finland	231	30.0

Source: "Diabetes Care" 1991.

Data interpolated from October 1992 "Scientific American" graph: error ±4 liters, error ±0.9 diabetes/100,000.

a) Graph a scatter plot with consumption as the independent variable (horizontal axis), and incidence number as the dependent variable (vertical axis).

b) Assume a linear model (a straight line) and "eye-ball" a best-fit line for the data.

c) According to your equation, how many liters of milk per year can safely be consumed? This can be read directly off the graph, or calculated from the answer in part b by setting the incidence number to zero.

d) What is the maximum number of ounces of milk that can be consumed per day based on your answer in part c? (One liter equals 1.0567 quarts)

e) What is the annual incidence for diabetes per 100,000 for a consumption rate of 250 liters per year according to your model?

f) How reliable is this value?

g) Does the data really represent a function since Canada and the United States both have the same independent variable paired with two different dependent variables, as do New Zealand and Denmark?

(Answers will vary depending on the best-fit estimate.)

Answers:

b) $y = .154x - 6.3$

c) 41 liters per year

d) 3.8 ounces

e) 32.2 diabetes/100,000

f) Since 250 liters per year is not too far removed from the Finland value, the resulting 32.2 diabetes/100,000 would not be an unreasonable extrapolation. Still, there is no way of really knowing (short of finding a country where the intake is 250 liters per year) without a better understanding of the human body. Additionally, common sense demands that the relationship cannot remain linear, since human beings do not have the capacity to drink endlessly.

g) Yes. If the association between the two variables was perfect (a straight line) it would mean there were no other effects influencing a child's disposition to developing diabetes. This is not the case. Other factors, such as genetics, will also play a role, but milk in the diet of children is still a strong enough factor to show an obvious trend. And it is with this trend line that the function is defined.

CHAPTER EIGHT

When Linearity Isn't Enough

The world curves, space warps, populations explode, and death abruptly halts a thousand unseen miracles—nothing in the physical world is linear. It is only humanity's lack of perception that has formed linear relationships out of the small piece of reality it is privy to.

Anyone who has ever traveled across the Texas Panhandle can appreciate why, for most of human history, the world was thought to be flat. The illusion is difficult to overcome when faced with a small view of a large landscape. The surface area of the Earth is roughly 2×10^8 square miles (two hundred million square miles). From a height of six feet above the Earth's surface we can see only an area of about thirty square miles. This perspective easily transforms the round Earth into a flat plane. Though such a conclusion is not unreasonable, careful observation suggests otherwise. Only the peak of a mountain is visible from a great distance, the rest is consumed by the curvature of the Earth. Likewise, ships far out at sea have hidden hulls, while full sails still remain in sight.

A circle is certainly far removed from a straight line and hence, definitely not linear. But imagine taking a very small segment out of a very large circle. If the small segment is seen in isolation, it can be mistakenly assumed a straight line. Everything depends upon how much of reality is accessible to measurement. The smaller the domain, the more accurately nonlinear relationships can be approximated with linear ones.

The word "domain" actually has a very precise mathematical definition. The domain represents all possible values for the independent variable x. Similarly, the "range" stands for all values of the dependent variable y. All functions have a domain and range whether they are linear or not.

In Problem 2 in Chapter Seven, the dependent variable (ppm of atmospheric carbon dioxide) is plotted against the independent variable of time. The domain covered 9 years [1959,1968] and the range 6.3 ppm [316.2,322.5]. The graph of this function is reproduced in Figure 8.1 with the dashed line representing linear extrapolations into the past and future where no data was originally given. On the same graph, more of the function is plotted over the enlarged domain [1959,1991].

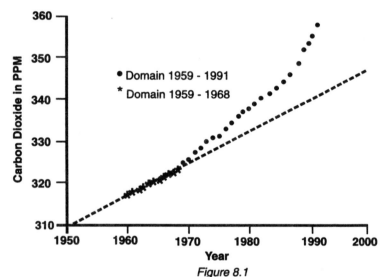

Figure 8.1
Atmospheric carbon dioxide concentration appears linear if viewed over the restricted domain 1959-1968. The dashed line represents the linear extrapolation of the restricted domain through the year 2000. Note how the actual data over the enlarged domain diverges from the linear model.

Source: Adapted from *Vital Signs 1992*
Worldwatch Insitute.

Clearly, the amount of atmospheric carbon dioxide has not been growing linearly with time. Therefore, any linear extrapolations of this function over more than a limited domain, would lead to ever increasing errors. Care must always be taken when using mathematical models to predict future trends. A mathematical model is not a complete description of reality; it represents a relationship between the variables that we have measured and our common sense understanding of the problem. To ask for more exceeds the bounds of the scientific method.

All of us have a tendency to reduce complex situations into simple models. These models may be adequate for small scale interpretations, but usually fail when extended. Perception without knowledge leads to dubious conclusions at best. As we have seen, circles become lines and spheres turn in to a planes. Additionally, a small life span, compared to epochs needed for biological and geological change, makes for an apparently static world. Our perception is constrained to the smallest tick of the cosmic clock. Connected events that span decades and centuries easily become isolated events to us. Small scale linear thinking sets in and the "big picture" is overlooked. If such were not the case, the environment would be healthy; a clear understanding between diet, health, and the environment would guide peoples' food choices; affordable health care would exist; and those polices that fostered our growing national debt would never have been implemented.

There is an interesting experiment called the Boiled Frog Syndrome.[1] It turns out that when a frog is placed in water and the temperature slowly increased, he is unable to detect any danger. Unless he is removed, he will remain in the water and eventually die. The same mind-set exists with cigarette smokers, drug users, and corporate polluters. The more narrow and linear a series of events appears to us, the less apt we are to take action. If negative change occurs too slowly, we do nothing but instinctively accommodate ourselves to an ever worsening situation.

Few times in human history has an understanding of nonlinear principles been so important. During the twentieth century we have been busy collecting data on the effects of industrialization on the ecosphere and on human health. We have learned that ecological changes do not follow linear sequential processes. Similarly, the biological changes which occur within each of us are also nonlinear. Regrettably, we have a difficult time perceiving, and hence understanding, these changes. A father dies at age sixty from a heart attack. Family, friends, and business associates are shocked because, "He was always so healthy and strong as an ox." But in addition to the stress at work, he ate lots of animal foods and smoked a few cigarettes each night. And then, after a particularly stressful morning at work, a hurried burger and fries for lunch, and a few cigarettes before retiring for the evening, the "straw that broke the camel's back" hit hard. The cumulative nonlinear effects of a lifetime of stress and bad habits precipitated the fatal heart attack. Processes in nature are similar. Nonlinearity and abrupt change are how nature defines itself, but such characteristics are never understood if the domain of observation is too narrow. How can scientists convince politicians and the general public of the seriousness of a situation, if deterioration initially appears modest? Without an appreciation of the true nature of change, and the mathematics that describe the rate of such change, linear thinking may result in ignoring timely precautions. In an age where massive oil spills, deforestations, and rapidly rising human population and resource consumption are common, understanding nonlinearity is essential.

The Parabola as an Example of Nonlinearity

Both linear and nonlinear functions can change quickly or slowly. The major difference is that linear functions have a constant rate of growth or decay, whereas nonlinear functions do not. The rate of change for a nonlinear function is itself always changing; additionally, this change may or may not be linear.

The salary example, $y = \$5.00t$, is a linear function because the rate of pay is constant at $5.00 per hour. Regardless of the number of hours worked, the pay rate remains $5.00 each hour. Figure 8.2a shows the rate of pay and Figure 8.2b shows the earnings.

The rate of pay graph is a horizontal line which means it is a constant function. One could think of this graph as analogously representing a constant speed of five miles per hour, and the earnings graph as the increasing distance traveled over an eight hour period at this constant rate. If we step on the accelerator the situation becomes nonlinear. As we accelerate, the distance traveled during each successive equal time interval grows larger, because the speed at which we travel continually increases. (Try constructing a table of values for figures 8.2a and 8.2b showing time, money earned and pay rate.)

Similarly, the linear earnings example of Figure 8.2b can be transformed into a nonlinear relationship by uniformly increasing the rate of pay by a fixed amount (say $5.00 per hour) every hour. It is important to understand what is meant by a "uniformly increasing rate." The pay rate does not abruptly change from $5.00/h to $10.00/h at the beginning of the second hour of work. Rather, the rate is smoothly and continuously changing from moment to moment, until at the beginning of the second hour it reaches a rate of $10.00/h. So the salary uniformly increases from an initial amount of $5.00/h, to $10.00/h, to $15.00/h, and so on, for each successive hour. Table 8.1 gives the earnings (middle column) and pay rate (last column) for an eight hour day.

Table 8.1

Earnings and pay rate over an eight hour period for a pay rate that begins at $5.00 per hour and is increased uniformly at $5.00 per hour every hour.

Time(hours)	Money Earned(dollars)	Pay Rate(dollars/h)
0	0.00	5
1	7.50	10
2	20.00	15
3	37.50	20

Time(hours)	Money Earned(dollars)	Pay Rate(dollars/h)
4	60.00	25
5	87.50	30
6	120.00	35
7	157.50	40
8	200.00	45

The equation describing the money earned is: $y = 2.5t^2 + 5t$, where y represents the earnings and t the time worked. For example, when t = 6 hours we substitute 6 for t which gives:
$2.5(6)^2 + 5(6) = 120$ dollars (see Table 8.1 above).

The equation for the rate of pay, however, is expressed by the linear equation: $y = 5t + 5$, where y represents the pay rate and t the time worked. Notice at t = 0 we get the initial condition that the pay rate is \$5.00/hour: $y = 5(0) + 5 = \$5.00$/hour.

It is a legitimate question to ask how the earnings equation is derived. Regrettably, the earnings equation is nonlinear and the derivation for such an equation requires considerable mathematical background. Readers who are up to the challenge are encouraged to read Appendix C. Fortunately, it is not necessary to understand the derivation for this equation in order to see the logic of its results. Since the pay rate changes uniformly, the average salary during the first hour of work is \$7.50/h (the average of \$5.00/h and \$10.00/h). Similarly, the average pay rate for the second time interval is \$12.50/h (the average of \$10.00/h and \$15.00/h). Since \$12.50 is earned during this time interval, the total money earned from the start of work through the second hour is \$7.50 + \$12.50 = \$20.00. The same line of reasoning will produce all the other values in the table.

Notice that the earnings equation has the squared term $2.5t^2$ in it. Such equations are called quadratic equations. The exact definition is: **an equation having a squared term as its largest power is called a second degree equation or quadratic equation. The graph of a quadratic equation is known as a parabola.** Any equation of the

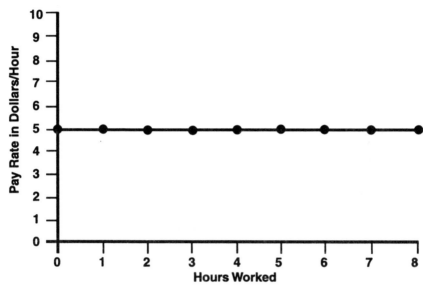

Figure 8.2a
Graph for a constant pay rate of $5.00 per hour

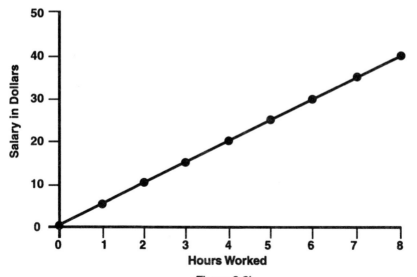

Figure 8.2b
Earnings increase linearly if the pay rate is constant

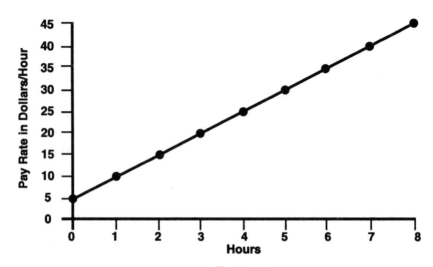

Figure 8.3a
Graph for a linear pay rate increasing $5.00 per hour each hour

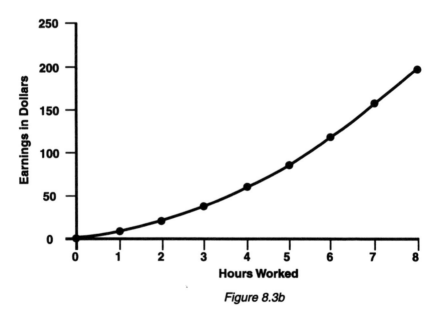

Figure 8.3b

Earnings increase quadratically if the pay
rate increases linearly.

form $ax^2 + bx + c$, (where a, b, and c are constants) is a parabola. In our example a = 2.5, b = 5, and c = 0 since there is no third term. As long as the constant "a" does not equal zero (even if b and c are zero) the equation remains a parabola. The graphs for the data in Table 8.1 are given in Figures 8.3a and 8.3b.

Previously, we likened our salary example to that of an accelerating car. There is a famous experiment that can also be explained using the same reasoning. In the last chapter we mentioned Galileo's experiment with falling objects. Table 8.2 shows the distance an object falls each second, and the speed it has reached at the end of each second of fall, over a time span of eight seconds. The data for this experiment is assumed to fit the condition for a "freely falling object." That is, the only force acting on the falling object is gravity—the effect of air resistance is ignored.

Table 8.2

Distance fallen and speed for a freely falling object.

Time(seconds)	Distance(feet)	Speed(ft/s)
0	0	0
1	16	32
2	64	64
3	144	96
4	256	128
5	400	160
6	576	192
7	784	224
8	1024	256

The equation that describes the distance fallen as a function of time is $d = 16t^2$ and the equation describing speed as a function of time is $s = 32t$. (See Appendix C for the derivation of $d = 16t^2$.) The first equation is a "second degree equation" (another name for a quadratic equation) where a = 16 and b = c = 0. The second equation is a

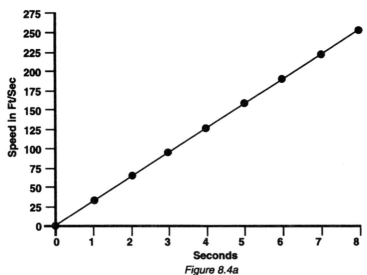

Figure 8.4a
The speed of a freely falling object increases linearly with time

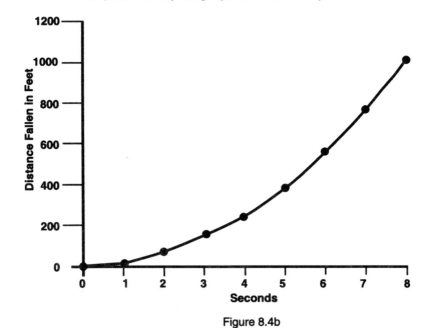

Figure 8.4b

The distance traveled by a free falling object
increases quadratically with time

"first degree equation" (another name for a linear equation) where m = 32 and b = 0. Their graphs are given in Figures 8.4b and 8.4a.

Notice how fast a freely falling object is going after only a few seconds. Since gravity accelerates objects so rapidly, Galileo could not gather experimental data by allowing objects to fall freely. Instead, he ingeniously realized he could measure the nature of falling objects equally well, by using inclined planes to reduce their speed.

Figure 8.4b is a parabola. Therefore, the mathematical model that describes a freely falling object when **time and distance** are measured, is a quadratic equation (nonlinear), and takes the form $ax^2 + bx + c$ (in the particular case above, b = c = 0). However, Figure 8.4a shows that a freely falling object, when **time and speed** are measured, is a linear equation, and so must have the form $y = mx + b$.

How is it that an accelerating car, an increasing pay scale, and a freely falling object all have the same mathematical form with respect to distance traveled, money earned, and distance fallen? (That is, they are all quadratic equations.) The key lies with the concept of a uniformly increasing rate. The earnings for a constant pay rate were linear. When the pay rate was changed so that it uniformly increased, the earnings became quadratic. The fact that the graph for a freely falling object is quadratic, suggests that its rate of fall must also be uniformly increasing.

Indeed, after the first second of fall, experiment shows a freely falling object has a speed of 32ft/s. By the end of the second second, the object's speed has uniformly increased to 64ft/s; by the end of the third second it is 96ft/s, and so on. So just as the salary rate increases by $5.00/h each hour, the falling object's rate increases by 32ft/s each second.

There is a slight difference in the form that the quadratic equations have for these two examples. In the salary example, the quadratic equation had two terms, a quadratic term ax^2 and a linear term bx, whereas the freely falling object example had only the quadratic term ax^2. The linear term arose in the salary example because we assumed an initial pay rate of $5.00/h. That is, at the moment work began, the salary was \$5.00/h. However, the freely falling object was assumed to be released from a state of rest, thus giving it an initial speed of zero feet per second. Had the object been given an initial upward or downward speed (if it had been thrown up or down, rather than released) the quadratic equation that described its motion would have had a linear term as well, which represented this initial condition.

Galileo's experiments led him to the correct conclusion that falling objects accelerate—that is, equal distances of fall do not occur with equal time increments. This is why the graph of distance versus time for a falling body is not linear. **In general, if a rate increases linearly with time, then the changing quantity will grow quadratically in time.**

The beauty in a mathematical equation is its universality. If two apparently different phenomena have the same mathematical form (linear, quadratic, etc.) then they behave similarly. Mathematics can render complex concepts into simple ones by the kind of analogies and generalizing principles discussed above. This, more than anything, is what makes the study of mathematics essential for the sciences. A secondary benefit is the possible cultivation of a broader, more holistic view for the individual—where superficial understanding is replaced by an appreciation of the underlying patterns governing nature.

Life in the Exponential Lane

The pace of life since the turn of the century has been dramatically increasing. Technological change, and with it the ability to manipulate our external environment, has profoundly altered how we live, what we need to know, and how we need to think. Since the Industrial Revolution began in the eighteenth century, the world has been experiencing rapid nonlinear growth and transformation. This is especially true of the last one hundred years. Things change so quickly today that the jobs we define ourselves by, the relationships we form, and the values we grew up with, seem to have no permanence. A mere decade leaves one generation out of touch with another, to the extent that we don't even listen to the same music.

Ten years ago I was an exploration geophysicist with a major oil company; today I am a teacher. Ten years ago my wife was married to an air traffic controller and kept house; today she is a registered nurse working with AIDS patients. Ten years ago few households owned a microwave oven, a VCR, or personal computer; today they are commonplace. Ten years ago the clear cutting of America's ancient forests was at best an obscure issue; today it gets headlines in newspapers. Ten years ago no one worried about the deficit; today America is a debtor nation. Ten years ago it was yuppies and stock options; today it's the environment and quality of life. Ten years ago only extremists cautioned against an animal-based diet; today almost everyone is watching their cholesterol count. Ten years ago the cost of health care was not a presidential campaign issue; today the First Lady is seeking congressional and industrial backing to attack the problem. Ten years ago there were eight hundred million fewer people on the planet, today there is less food and less clean water. Ten years ago few people worried about AIDS; today many grade-schoolers are being taught about the use of condoms. Ten years ago few of us knew about the holes in the ozone layer around the polar regions; today we have advertising promoting sunscreen lotion and sunglasses that block ultraviolet radiation. Ten years ago nuclear war seemed inevitable; today the Soviet Union has collapsed and Russia is moving toward a western style economy and government. The list goes on and on.

Linearity in today's world is an archaic concept. Even the parabola is left in the dust of the crazy pace of the twentieth century. We need a new view, a different mathematical model capable of accurately describing the events unfolding today. More importantly, we need to turn the mathematics upon ourselves, to see where we have been, and where we are headed.

During previous centuries, mathematics explained the workings of the natural world—the orbits of planets, the fall of a rain drop, the

propagation of sound and light. But throughout the twentieth century we have accumulated data about ourselves and the effects we are
having on our planet. The interpretation of much of this data
requires the use of exponential functions.

The Exponential Function

Thus far we have looked at linear and quadratic growth. Linear
growth occurs when the rate of growth is constant. Quadratic growth
is recognized when the rate of growth uniformly (linearly) changes.
In general, this pattern could be continually extrapolated. For
instance, if the pay rate grew quadratically in our salary example, the
earnings would grow as a "third order equation" (that is, an equation
having a cubic term, x^3 , as the highest power). Similarly, if the pay
rate grew cubicly the earnings would obey a "fourth order equation."

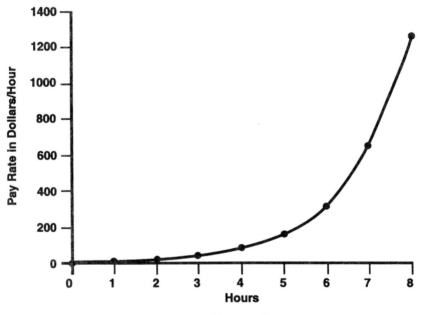

Figure 8.5a
Graph of an exponential pay rate

The pattern that emerges describes the pay rate with an "nth order equation" and the earnings with an "(n+1)th order equation," where n is any whole number. (Recall that "order" represents the highest power in the equation.) Yet regardless of how high n is permitted to be for the above kind of function (which is called a **polynomial function**), the exponential function still has the capacity for greater growth. We will see that for the exponential function, both the pay rate and earnings grow exponentially.

Using our salary example again, assume an initial pay rate of $5.00 per hour. This time, however, we let the pay rate change continuously such that the rate doubles by the end of each hour. That is, by the end of the first hour the pay rate has reached $10.00/h, by the end of the second hour, it is $20.00/h, the third hour, $40.00/h, and so forth. Table 8.3 shows the values for earnings and pay rate over an eight hour period.

Table 8.3

Earnings and pay rate for exponential growth.

Time(hours)	Earnings(dollars)	Pay Rate(dollars/h)
0	0	5
1	7.21	10
2	21.64	20
3	50.49	40
4	108.20	80
5	223.61	160
6	454.49	320
7	916.11	640
8	1839.43	1280

The function that describes the pay rate (Figure 8.5a) is $y = 5(2^x)$. That is, if x = 6, we have: $5(2^6) = 5(2 \times 2 \times 2 \times 2 \times 2 \times 2) = \$320/h$. The part of the equation that has a constant raised to a variable (2^x) is what governs the function and what is meant by "exponential

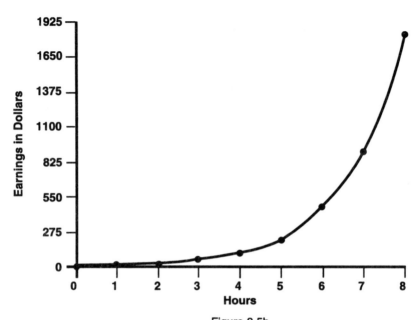

Figure 8.5b
The earnings derived from an
exponential pay rate are also exponential

behavior."

The equation for the earnings (Figure 8.5b) is $y = 7.21(2^x - 1)$. Therefore, when $x = 6$, the function is evaluated as $y = 7.21(2^6 - 1)$, which equals: $7.21(2 \times 2 \times 2 \times 2 \times 2 \times 2 - 1)$, which is, $7.21 \times 63 = \$454.23$. (The error in the cents (see Table 8.3) occurs because 7.21 is an approximation.)

The 7.21 in the equation above must appear quite unusual. It arises because the changing pay rate is not linear. Therefore, the "average" pay rate for any one hour interval, cannot be calculated by averaging the values at the beginning and end of each interval. This is not only true for the exponential case, but for any polynomial where the pay rate is not linear. Graphically, this makes sense because for a linear pay rate the midpoint (the average rate) for any two points on the line is also on the line. This is not generally true for a nonlinear rate. Consider a pay rate that grows quadratically to illustrate this point. The center (average value) of a straight line drawn between any two points on the graph of a quadratic does not fall on the quadratic. Hence, the idea of averaging like this for nonlinear functions is meaningless. Such reasoning is analogous to assuming that if you travel for five minutes at thirty miles per hour and three hours at sixty miles per hour, your average speed for the total trip is forty-five miles per hour!

Once the constant 7.21 is evaluated (see Appendix C), we need only double each of the earnings and add them to the wages of the previous hour in order to find the earned money. For instance, the earnings from zero hours to the end of the first hour are $7.21. Doubling this number gives $14.42. This represents the money earned during the second hour of work, and therefore, the total wage from the start of the day through the second hour is $7.21 + $14.42 = $21.63 (again the slight difference of a penny arises due to round-off error—see Table 8.3 page 165). Continuing in the same manner (next double $14.42 and add this result to all the previous money earned), we would eventually generate all the values for the earnings given in Table 8.3.

In the previous example, starting with $5.00/h put a constraint on successive pay rates while generating an exponential function. The very nature of an exponential function depends on some initial quantity. For example, when cells begin to multiply, the initial amount will determine the number at any future time. If the population in question doubles over each time increment, as in cell mitosis, the growth would follow an exponential function of the form $P = P_i(2^t)$—where P is the population at any time, P_i is the initial population, and t is time. At time t = 0, the population is set at P_i (since $2^0 = 1$). All future populations will be dependent upon P_i and the exponential growth of 2^t.

We often associate exponential growth with the concept of doubling. Though this is sometimes true, it is a special case of an exponential function, not the only one available. Consider the exponential function $y = 3^x$. Such a function generates the values: 1,3,9,27,81,.... Here each successive value is three times the previous

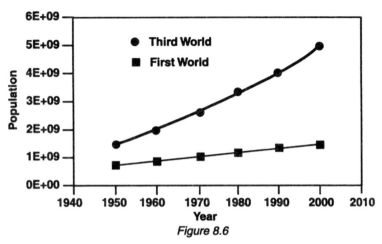

Figure 8.6

First World population growth is linear over the given
time span whereas Third World population is exponential.

Source: Adapted from, *Atlas of the Environment*

one.

In general, any equation of the form $y = y_i(b^{kx})$—where y_i is a constant designating an initial amount, b is a constant representing the factor by which growth is occurring, x is a variable (usually given in units of time) and k is a constant—is an exponential function.

*   *   *

Figure 8.6 is a graph showing population growth for both the First and Third Worlds. (The y-axis is given in scientific notation where, for example, "6E+09" is read 6×10^9). The rate of First World growth over the domain [1950,2000] has been, and is predicted to continue growing linearly through the year 2000. By using methods from Chapter Seven, we can find an equation which describes the rate of population for this period. But the rate of Third World growth is definitely not linear; it can be shown to follow an exponential curve (see Appendix C).

*   *   *

Exponential functions can also be used to represent decay as well as growth; radioactive materials are a good example of this. Figure 8.7 shows the decay curve for Cesium 137, a radioactive material, which is used in cancer therapy.

The equation for Figure 8.7 is $y = y_i(2^{-t/30})$, where t is time in years, y_i the initial quantity of Cesium 137, and y the amount of material left after a time t. Note that at t = 30 years, the amount of Cesium 137 remaining is half of the initial value (recall $2^{-1} = 1/2$). Thirty years is therefore the "half-life" of Cesium 137. The problem with many radioactive materials is that their half-life can be centuries. Some of the radioactive waste we are creating today will still be haz-

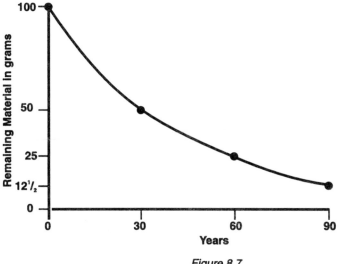

Figure 8.7

An example of exponential decay—Radioactive Cesium 137 with an intial amount of 100 grams.

ardous hundreds of years from now.

Figure 8.8 is a graph showing the three functions we have discussed so far—linear, quadratic, and exponential. There is, at times,

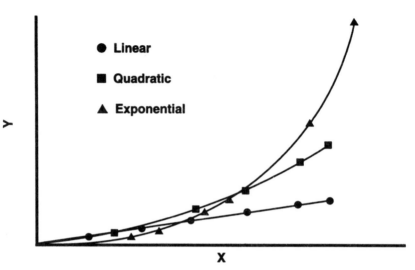

Figure 8.8
Comparison of linear, quadratic, and exponential growth

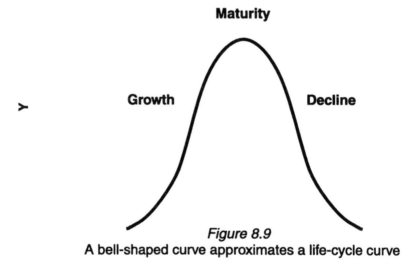

Figure 8.9
A bell-shaped curve approximates a life-cycle curve

confusion over the fact that quadratic functions are not exponential functions. A quadratic function has exponents, as do all polynomial functions, but the exponents are constants. Exponential functions have exponents which are variables, and therefore grow or decay exponentially.

Notice how all three functions increase without bound, yet nothing in nature increases forever. Most things grow, mature, and die. This is true of organic life-cycles, or the life-cycles of resource use, technological innovation, or the creative output of scientists and artists.[2] Consider Figure 8.9 which is commonly referred to as a bell-shaped curve.

We can use this curve to make a point regarding growth, maturity, and decline. Finite "resources" like oil, ancient forests, and whales, are subject to increasing use until their consumption is maximized. If the demand continues, and the resource is still exploited, production will decline and the resource will be exhausted. Creative output follows a similar path. There is usually a start-up period, followed by increasing output that reaches a ceiling of maximum productivity. Afterwards, output tapers off, and a complete cessation of activity occurs with death. Many new products in the marketplace follow a similar life-cycle.

Fads fit exceptionally well into this model also. The hula-hoops of the 1950s and 1960s, and the mood rings, pet rocks, and leisure suits of the 1970s are a few examples of such fads.

Fads spread like diseases, quite literally. There is usually an initial slow-to-modest growth period until the item "catches-on," after which growth rapidly takes off, until reaching some maximum level. Soon after this, interest in the item wanes and the number sold begins to decline quickly, until sales diminish to some nominal level. Items that have longevity, like television sets, follow the same beginning but do not fade out as dramatically as do fad items.

Within a year or two after telephone answering machines went on the market, everyone I knew purchased one. The same has been true of VCRs and computers. Each item has a respective "niche" to fill. The buying frenzy for all new innovations slows down when everyone who is going to buy the item already has. Afterwards sales level off, fueled by replacement items and the next generation who purchases their own.

After the item fills its niche, the rapid growth it enjoyed is over; though it may continue growing as the "need" for the item persists with increasing population. But given enough time, any item will eventually become extinct. Phonograph records are a good example of this. The invention of the phonograph created a market for records that spanned about seventy years. But the compact disc, a more successful competitor, overtook the niche of the vinyl record. Records themselves have been subjected to evolutionary changes, where one form died out in place of another. The first disk records were made from metal and sprayed with vinyl. Later "generations" were made with 100 percent vinyl, and continued to became more flexible. But it has been only within the last few years that records as a "species" have stopped reproducing (numerically) because of competition from the more successful compact disk.

The bell-shaped curve in Figure 8.9 can be used to generate a logistic function, also called an S-curve. **An S-curve shows the total accumulation from the life-cycle curve and therefore never diminishes.** (Bell-shaped curves or "normal" distributions are not exactly the same as a true life-cycle curve, but the difference for our purposes is negligible.)

Theodore Modis has a section in his book *Predictions* entitled, "Man-made Dinosaurs," where he discusses the life-cycles of such things as supertankers, Gothic cathedrals, and particle accelerators. Particle accelerators are used to investigate the creation and decay of subatomic particles. Each of these innovations has completed its life-cycle; the only exception possibly being the particle accelerator wherein the potential for one or two more still exists.[3]

Supertankers will serve as a representative example for explaining Modis's "Man-made Dinosaurs." During the 1970s, ships called supertankers were constructed with a carrying capacity of more than three hundred thousand tons. But over a period of ten years or so, competition with smaller ships showed they were not capable of holding their own in the marketplace. The 1980s and 1990s have witnessed them steadily being replaced by the smaller vessels. It will not be many more years before the last of the ships are decommissioned.[4]

Figure 8.10a shows the life-cycle curve for supertankers and Figure 8.10b shows its corresponding S-curve.[5]

At the beginning of the innovation's life, growth was modest and so the S-curve rose slowly. As the innovation caught on, the **cumulative number** of ships increased rapidly and the S-curve rose more sharply. In the final part of its life-cycle, less and less were produced and the corresponding growth of its S-curve flattened out. The final part of the curve has approached a limiting value which can be thought of as the niche capacity for the innovation.

S-curves are another example of an exponential function. One way to represent them mathematically is with the equation $y = M/[1+A(2^{-at})]$, where M is a constant denoting the niche capacity, A and a are constants found from the initial conditions of the problem, and t is time. S-curves are used to explore social and commercial trends. These trends are often helpful in analyzing human behavior on a macroscopic scale. They also lend insight into the productivity of individuals and their ultimate potential. The idea of personalizing S-curves to individuals is really the work of Cesare Marchetti. As Modis explains in his book:

> Cesare Marchetti was the first to associate the evolution of a person's creativity and productivity with natural growth. He assumed that a work of art or science is the final expression of a 'pulse of action' that originates somewhere in the depths of the brain and works its way through all intermediate stages to produce a creation. He then studied the number of these creations over time and found that its growth follows S-curves. Each curve presupposed a final target, a niche size he called a perceived target, since competition may prevent one from reaching it. He then proceeded to study hundreds of well-documented artists and scientists. In each case he took the total number of creations known for each of these people, graphed them over time, and determined the S-curve that would best connect these data points. He found that most people died close to

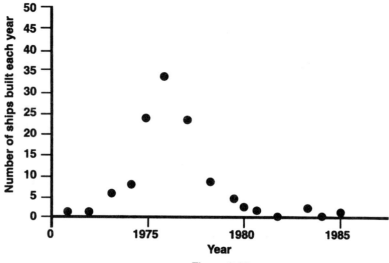

Figure 8.10a

The rate of growth for supertankers approximates a
bell-shaped curve

Source: Adapted from *Predictions*

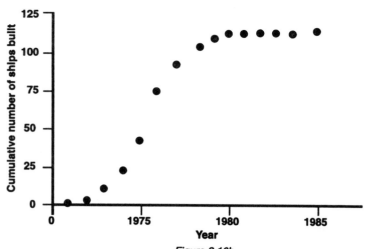

Figure 8.10b

The cumulative growth of supertankers follows an S-curve

Source: Adapted from *Predictions*

having realized their perceived potential.[6]

Marchetti believes that most people develop somewhere between 90 to 100 percent of their potential, and even those who die young (like Mozart who died at thirty-five), do so because they have nothing left to say.[7] There is the implication in both the work of Modis and Marchetti that "temporal age" may be only one form of aging, and we need also to consider "creative age." From this point of view, Mozart died young chronologically but old creatively. Modis seems to accept this though his own research allows for accidents—as in the case of the poet Percy Bysshe Shelley, who died at age thirty after having completed only half of his S-curve. Modis also makes an argument that suicide may play a role in a person's life when they are creatively exhausted.

There is a ring of predestination in both the work of Modis and Marchetti that some may find intellectually troubling. Their work may make more sense if we compare their views on creative output to biological output.

Genetically, every living thing from an oak tree to a human being is programmed to reach its optimum height, given the proper environment in which to do so. By extending this idea to creativity, Modis and Marchetti are showing a psychic analogue to biological programming. Such an idea is not so unreasonable. We may, after all, intuitively realize this each time we make reference to an individual not fulfilling their potential. Indeed, from an educational point of view, it supports the value of optimizing a child's home and school environment so that nurture may work hand in hand with nature.

In a sense we have come full cycle. How much mathematics we really do need to know, ultimately depends upon the life-cycle of the society we inhabit. Collectively, we are each part of the ebb and flow of the events that shape our society. Any means available to us to gain a greater understanding of ourselves is beneficial.

Mathematics is an essential tool in this quest given the present evolution of our culture. It is an important piece in the complex tapestry of the civilization that each of us has inherited. We owe it to ourselves and our children to insure that no subject of human knowledge is accessible only to a chosen few.

Epilogue

What will the world be like in a hundred years? This is a question often answered by science-fiction writers. For as dramatic as the changes have been over the last ten decades, the next century will undoubtedly place us politically, socially, and technologically far beyond any conceived fiction

Though nothing is certain, we do know that education has always been a prerequisite for evolving societies. As a result of this, numeracy beyond arithmetic will be essential for the average person and the growth of any future society which that person inhabits. Yet if fundamental changes do not occur in American education, we will continue to grow into a more polarized society. We will be a nation dangerously divided into know and know-nots, into understand and understand-nots, into knowing-how-to-learn and knowing-how-to-learn-nots.

We must fully appreciate that we no longer live in simple times. We do not engage in barter and few of us live off the land. Roman soldiers were paid in salt for their service; well into the eighteenth century, tobacco served as money; British coal workers were partly paid in beer until the late nineteenth century. But we live in a different era and ascribe to a different mind-set today. In the world of the "global village," each person who shares in a participatory government takes on universal responsibilities. This is the first time in history that so many have the potential to be heard. Yet no democratic society can exist without an educated population.

The approaching new century will place greater academic demands upon each American, if we wish to continue living in a free society with a first-rate life-style. We cannot afford to allow the educational chasm between the members of our society to grow wider. If we do, future generations may inhabit a bizarre world, characterized by enormous technological sophistication with ever increasing mass illiteracy—a "brown age," if you will. Such is the possibility if we continue issuing university degrees to adults who are fearful of seventh-grade arithmetic.

No society can fully mature without recognizing that each of its members are unique, and hence have different talents to contribute for the growth of the collective culture. If we succeed in making education relevant, if we embrace the whole person in learning, if education truly becomes universal, then the next century will be better for all of us.

Appendix A
Different Bases

Writing numbers in different bases can be readily understood by examining how numbers in base 10 are written. Consider the number 1,251. This means: 1 one-thousand, 2 one-hundreds, 5 tens, and 1 one.

With the concept of place-value we can construct a table showing the placement for each of these numbers.

Decimal Table

Thousands	Hundreds	Tens	ones
10x10x10	10x10	10	1
10^3	10^2	10^1	10^0
1	**2**	**5**	**1**

Notice that each column above can be written as increasing multiples of ten (powers of ten)—see Chapter Five, page 82. The same pattern can be used to express any number in any base. To write the number 1,251 in base 2 we form columns of numbers with increasing powers of 2.

Binary Table

2^{10}	2^9	2^8	2^7	2^6	2^5	2^4	2^3	2^2	2^1	2^0
1	0	0	1	1	1	0	0	0	1	1

Therefore the binary number for 1,251 is 10011100011. (The term binary is used for base two.) This is what's happening: There is one 2^{10}(1024) in 1,251. If we subtract 1,024 from 1,251 we have 227. But there is one 2^7(128) in 227. Subtracting 128 from 227 gives 99. There is one 2^6(64) in 99. Subtracting 64 from 99 gives 35. There is one 2^5(32) in 35. Subtracting 32 from 35 gives 3. There is one 2^1(2) in 3. Subtracting 2 from 3 gives 1, and there is one 1 in 2^0.

We do exactly the same thing in order to write a number in base ten. How many 10^3(1,000's) in 1,251? One. We subtract 1,000 from 1,251 which gives 251. How many 10^2(100's) in 251? Two. We subtract 200 from 251 which gives 51. How many 10^1(10's) in 51? Five. We subtract 50 from 51 which gives 1. How many 10^0(1) in 1? One.

Regardless of the base a number is expressed in, the same pattern is followed. For example, to express a number in base 3 we would construct a similar place-value system using powers of three. Verify for yourself that 1,251 in base 3 is 1201100.

*   *   *

In Chapter 5, example 3, you were shown how to calculate percent profit. Actually, there is more than one definition used to calculate this value. The method shown in Chapter 5 was: (profit in dollars/cost to seller) × 100. Using this definition, it makes no sense to assume that the seller's cost was ever zero. If it were, you would be dividing by zero which would yield an undefined (infinite) percent profit. In a typical business transaction there would always be a cost to the seller. However, confusion may arise when, on a personal level, an item is obtained without cost (an inheritance, a gift, a lucky find, etc.) What then?

Here we have another definition available to us: (profit in dollars/selling price) × 100. Using this definition the denominator can never be zero, nor can the percent profit ever be greater than 100 percent.

Appendix B
The Population Surveyed

Total population surveyed: 102
Age range: 21-72
Median age: 33
Income: Over two-thirds earned annual salaries of at least $20,000.
Sex: 57 females and 45 males
Education: All completed at least 4 years of college. 32 females and 24 males had completed at least one year of graduate studies. No one with a degree in mathematics, engineering, or physics was given the test.
Race: All but two were Caucasian.

Testing Conditions

Time allotted: As much as needed
Place: Local coffee houses in the New Orleans area
Calculators: Not permitted

The Test

Ten questions were given requiring competency in seventh grade arithmetic. Problems ranged from simple addition with whole numbers to fraction addition with unlike denominators. The results of problem #3 (200/.8) are suspect because 29 out of 51 who incorrectly answered problem #3 gave the answer as 25 instead of 250 (see the next page for the test). There is the strong possibility that many failed to see the decimal point in the problem.

The test is reproduced below.

Survey

Age_____ sex _____ Profession _____

Income:

$0-$10,000 $10,000-$15,000 $15,000-$20,000
$20,000-$25,000 $25,000-$35,000   above $35,000

Education * (circle one):
K   1   2   3   4   5   6   7   8   9   10   11   12
College 1   2   3   4   Graduate 1   2   3   4   5
Degree(s) Earned _____
Major(s) _____

Please answer all questions to the best of your ability. No calculators are permitted. If needed, use any free space for scratch work on this paper.

1. 15 + 43 = _____

2. 17.09 + 14.8 = _____

3. 200 ÷ .8 = _____

4. 8.5 × 9.2 = _____

5. 2/7 + 4/9 = _____

6. $3/8 \times 5/11 =$ _____

7. $1/3$ of $1/12 =$ _____

8. $2/7 \div 4/9 =$ _____

9. 25% of 80 = _____

10. 8% of $6.00 = _____

* *Only those surveys with at least four years of college were used. (See next page for answers.)*
The results for all 102 participates are provided in Table form below and in Appendix B Figures 1-5.

Table B1

Problem Number	Number Answered Incorrectly
1	1
2	14
3	51 [22] 1*
4	26
5	46
6	27
7	40 2*
8	42
9	6
10	25

The answers to the test are:

1) 58   2) 31.89   3) 250   4) 78.2   5) 46/63   6) 15/88
7) 1/36   8) 18/28 or 9/14   9) 20   10) 48¢

*[1] See comment on previous page regarding problem #3.
*[2] 3 out of the 102 tests did not include this problem.

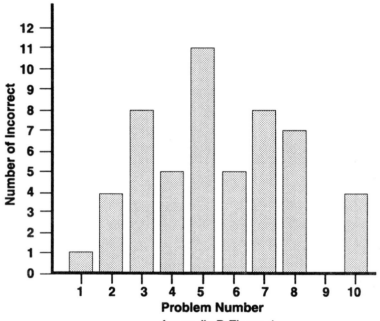

Appendix B Figure 1
Statistics for 21 males with four years of college.

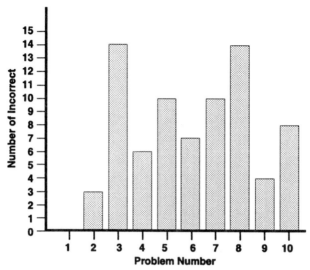

Appendix B Figure 2
Statistics for 25 females with four years of college.

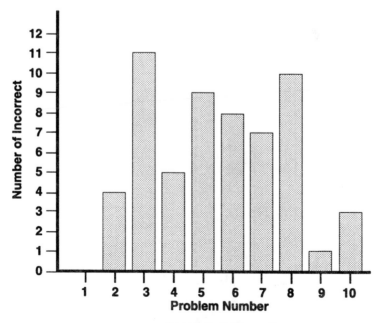

Appendix B Figure 3
Statistics for 24 males with more than four years of college.

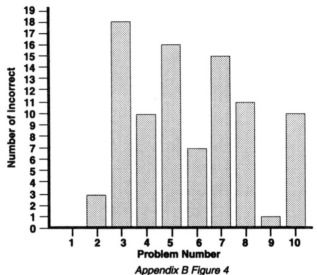

Appendix B Figure 4
Statistics for 32 females with more than four years of college.

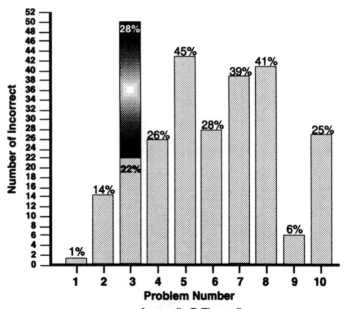

Appendix B Figure 5
Cumulative statistics for all four groups (102 people surveyed).

Appendix C
Deriving the Equations in Chapter Eight

The derivations for several of the equations in Chapter Eight exceeded what I considered the average readers' mathematical knowledge. An explanation of these equations for the novice would have been too long and involved. (Concepts such as simultaneous solutions of equations, logarithms, and calculus must be clearly understood.) I therefore present the derivations of these equations below in the order in which they appeared within the book and assume the reader is familiar with the above concepts. The derivations presented in this appendix are those that I believe are the most straight forward. They are not intended to be the only solutions, indeed the reader may wish to find other insightful solutions.

* * *

On page 156 the equation $y = 2.5t^2 + 5t$ is given for hypothetical earnings assuming a linear pay rate that increases \$5.00/h every hour. Two possible derivations for the above equation can be done as follows: solution of simultaneous equations, and the integration of $y = 5t + 5$. Both cases are shown below, respectively.

Case 1:

The general form of the quadratic equation is:
$f(x) = ax^2 + bx + c$

Table 8.1 gives $f(0) = 0$, $f(1) = 7.5$, and $f(2) = 20$. $f(0) = 0$ gives the value of the c as 0 ($0 = a(0) + b(0) + c$).

$f(1)$ and $f(2)$ are used to generate two equations in two unknowns:
$f(1) = 7.5 = a(1) + b(1) = a + b$
$f(2) = 20 = a(2) + b(2) = 4a + 2b$, therefore our two equations are:
$7.5 = a + b$
$20 = 4a + 2b$
The solution for this set of simultaneous equations is (2.5,5), hence $a = 2.5$ and $b = 5$. Knowing $a = 2.5$, $b = 5$ and $c = 0$, we can write the quadratic equation $y = 2.5t^2 + 5t$.

Case 2:

The problem can also be solved by integrating the equation: $y = 5t + 5$. Since y represents the rate at which the earnings are acquired (the pay rate) we can express y as de/dt where e represents the earnings. The equation we need to integrate is therefore:
$\int de = \int (5t + 5)dt$
The right side of the equation integrates out to $2.5t^2 + 5t$. The initial condition: the earnings $= 0$ ($e = 0$) when $t = 0$, gives 0 for the constant of integration—which is the constant c in the quadratic equation. Once again our solution is $y = 2.5t^2 + 5t$, by a change of variable name.

*   *   *

On page 159 the distance a freely falling object falls as a function of time is given as $d = 16t^2$. Using the same two methods described above we can quickly arrive at this equation. For the first method we use Table 8.2.

At $t = 0$ seconds the distance fallen is 0 feet, so:
$0 = a(0) + b(0) + c$, therefore $c = 0$ feet
Similarly, for $t = 1$ second, $d = 16$ feet, so:
$16 = a(1) + b(1)$, and for $t = 2$ seconds, $d = 64$ feet, so $64 = a(2) +$

b(2) = 4a + 2b, therefore our two equations are:

16 = a + b

64 = 4a + 2b

Solving the two equations simultaneously gives b = 0 and a = 16. Hence, d = 16t². Similarly, evaluating $\int dx = \int 32t\,dt$ gives the same results (where the speed = $^{dx}/_{dt}$).

Let s = dx/dt, then: dx = 32t dt. The integral $\int 32t\,dt$ is 16t². The constant of integration equals zero since x = 0 when t = 0. The final equation is therefore, x = 16t², or as before, by changing the variable name d = 16t².

*   *   *

On page 166 we are given the equation y = 7.21(2^X-1) as the earnings for the exponential pay rate y = 5(2^X). The same methods can be used again to derive the first equation. However, integration of y = 5(2^X) will provide for a more accurate answer since the 7.21 is an approximation. In general, the integral of an exponential function $\int a^x dx$ evaluates to: a^x(1/ln a) + C, where ln is the natural log, a for our case is 2, and C is the constant of integration. 1 divided by the natural log of 2 (1/ln2) = 1.442695041.... This number is multiplied by the constant 5 which gives 7.213475205..., hence the constant 7.21 in the equation above. Our equation is therefore: y = 7.21(2^X) + C (rounding-off 7.213475205...). Table 8.3 shows that when t = 0, y = 0. Plugging these values into the above equation gives, C = -7.21, which yields, y = 7.21(2^X) - 7.21, and upon factoring out the 7.21, leaves us with y = 7.21(2^X- 1).

*   *   *

Figure 8.6, page 168, shows Third World population as a non-linear function. If Third World population is plotted on semi-log paper the data will straighten out into an essentially linear looking relationship between time and population growth. This shows that

Third World population has and is expected to continue growing exponentially over the domain [1950,2000]. (If log paper is not available, the data can be linearized by taking the logarithm of dependent variable and plotting it against the independent variable.)

Footnotes

Chapter One—The Problem

1 Colin Wilson, *New Pathways in Psychology*: Maslow and the Post-Freudian Revolution (New York: Mentor, 1974), p. 12.

Chapter Two—Those We Leave Behind

1 Jonathan Kozol, *Savage Inequalities* (New York: Crown, 1991), p. 149.

2 Kozol, pp. 26, 58, 68-69, 224, 231.

3 Kozol, p. 58.

4 Kozol, p. 118.

5 Gail Collins and Dan Collins, *The Millennium Boo*k (New York: Doubleday, 1991), p. 50.

6 Paul Hewitt (Lecturer), "*Conceptual Physics with Hewitt: Polarized Light and 3-D Viewing*," (Addison-Wesley, 1987).

7 Tobias Dantzig, *Number: The Language of Science* (4th ed., rev.) (Garden City, New York: Doubleday, 1954), p. ix.

8 Arthur Fisher, "*Crisis in Education: Part One*," Popular Science, August, 1992, p. 60.

9 Fisher, p. 60.

10 Fisher, p. 59.

11 Robert W. May, "*How Many Species Inhabit the Earth?*," Scientific American, October 1992.

12 John W. Wright, General Editor, *The Universal Almanac* 1991 (Kansas City: Andrews and McMeel, 1990), p. 269.

13 John Allen Paulos, *Innumeracy: Mathematical Illiteracy and Its Consequences* (New York: Hill and Wang, 1988), p. 5.

14 Paulos, p. 122.

15 Ian Stewart, *Game, Set and Math: Enigmas and Conundrums* (London: Penguin, 1991), p. vii.

Chapter Three—A Brief History of Mathematics

1 Graham Flegg, *Numbers: Their History and Meaning* (London: Andre Deutsch Limited, 1983), p. 41.

2 Tobias Dantzig, *Number: The Language of Science* (4th ed., rev.) (Garden City, New York: Doubleday, 1954), pp. 21-22.

3 Flegg, p. 45.

4 George Gamow, *One Two Three ... Infinity: Facts and Speculations of Science* (New York: Mentor, 1953), p. 15.

5 Flegg, p. 19.

6 Flegg, p. 36.

7 Petr Beckmann, *A History of Pi* (New York: St. Martin's, 1971), p. 23.

8 Beckmann, p. 23. See also: Dirk J. Struik, *A Concise History of Mathematics* (3rd ed., rev.) (New York: Dover, 1966), p. 20. Struik states there were 85 problems.

9 Flegg, p. 94.

10 Florian Cajori, *"The Egyptians,"* in *Growth of Mathematics: From Counting to Calculus* ed. Robert W. Marks (New York: Bantam, 1964), p. 87.

11 Flegg, p. 60.

12 Cajori, p. 87.

13 Flegg, p. 252 and Cajori, p.81.

14 Cajori, p. 81.

15 Gail Collins and Dan Collins, *The Millennium Book* (New York: Doubleday, 1991), p. 62

16 John Perlin, *A Forest Journey: The Role of Wood in the Development of Civilization* (New York: Norton, 1989), p. 132.

17 Charles Van Doren, *A History of Knowledge: The Pivotal Events, People, and Achievements of World History* (New York: Ballantine, 1991), p. 10.

18 Norman Angell, *The Story of Money* (Garden City, New York: Garden City Publishing Company, Inc., 1929.), p. 31.

19 Angell, p. 36.

20 Elgin Groseclose, *Money and Man: A Survey of Monetary Experience* (New York: Frederick Ungar Publishing Co., 1961), p.16

21 Groseclose, p. 18.

22 Struik, p. 41.

23 Collins, p. 32.

24 Groseclose, p. 33.

25 Collins, p. 23.

26 Struik, p. 84.

27 Timothy Ferris, *Coming of Age in the Milky Way* (New York: Morrow, 1988), p. 56.

28 Daniel J. Boorstin, *The Discoverers* (New York: Vintage, 1985), p. 56.

29 Ferris, p. 22.

30 Boorstin, p. 230.

31 Boorstin, p. 49.

32 Dennis W. Richardson, *Evolution of an Electronic Funds Transfer System* (Cambridge, Massachesetts: Colonial Press Inc., 1970), p. 19.

Chapter Four—Numbers for the Nineties

1 Philip J. Davis and Reuben Hersh, *The Mathematical Experience* (Boston: Houghton Mifflin Company, 1981), p. 98.

2 Theodore Modis, *Predictions* (New York: Simon and Schuster, 1992), p. 30. See also: Charles Panati, *Panati's Extraordinary Endings of Practically Everything and Everybody* (New York: Harper and Row, 1989), p. 172.

3 Modis, p. 30.

4 Samuel Glasstone, *Sourcebook on the Space Sciences* (Princeton, New Jersey: Van Nostrand, 1965), p. 814.

5 Lester R. Brown, Christopher Flavin, and Hal Kane, *Vital Signs 1992: The Trends That Are Shaping Our Future* (New York: Norton, 1992), p. 80.

6 John W. Wright, General Editor, *The Universal Almanac 1991* (Kansas City: Andrews and McMeel, 1990), p. 281.

7 Brown, p. 80.

8 Wright, p. 281.

9 John Robbins, "Realities for the 90's" excerpted from (Walpole, New Hampshire: Stillpoint, 1987), p.4.

10 Alan Durning, *How Much Is Enough?* (New York: Norton, 1992), p. 71.

11 Durning, p. 72.

12 Brown, p. 71.

13 John Feltman, Editor, *Prevention Magazine's Giant Book of Health Facts* (New York: Rodale, 1991), p. 115.

14 George J. Demko with Jerome Agel and Eugene Boe, *Why in the World: Adventures in Geography* (New York: Doubleday, 1992), p. 125

15 Durning, p. 95.

16 Durning, p. 76.

17 Brown, pp. 44-47.

18 Demko, p. 385.

19 United States Department of Agriculture, *Agricultural Statistics 1992*, (Washington D.C.: Government Printing Office), p. 341.

20 United States Department of Health and Human Services, *"Facts About Blood Cholesterol,"* (Washington D.C.: Government Printing Office, October 1990), pp. 12-13.

21 Demko, p. 386.

22 Wright, p. 307.

23 Demko, p. 166.

24 Geoffrey Lean, Don Hinrichsen, and Adam Markham, *Atlas of*

the *Enviromnent* (New York: Prentice Hall Press, 1990), p. 20.

25 Demko, p. 25.

26 Durning, p. 26.

27 Lean, p. 44.

28 Demko, p. 166.

29 Robbins, "*Realities for the 90's*," p. 4.

30 Catherine Lerza and Michael Jacobson, *Food for People, Not for Profit: A Sourcebook on the Food Crisis* (New York: Ballantine, 1975), pp. 235-236.

31 Robbins, "*Realities for the 90's*," p. 5. (Robbins's calculation predicts 100,000,000.)

32 Robbins, "*Realities for the 90's*," p. 5.

33 Robbins, "*Realities for the 90's*," p. 5.

34 Robbins, "*Realities for the 90's*," p. 5.

35 Robbins, "*Realities for the 90's*," p. 5.

36 John W. Firor, "*Global Heating: The Greenhouse Effect*," Louisiana Conservationist, January/February 1989.

37 Brown, p. 60.

38 World Resources Institute, *Environmental Almanac* (New York: Houghton Mifflin, 1991), p. 277.

39 World Resources Institute, p. 140.

40 Lean, p. 96.

41 Lean, p. 93.

42 World Resources Institute, p. 279.

43 Robert M. May, "How Many Species Inhabit the Earth?," *Scientific American*, October 1992.

44 World Resources Institute, p. 285.

45 Al Gore, *Earth in the Balance: Ecology and the Human Spirit* (New York: Houghton Mifflin, 1992), p. 139.

46 Wright, p. 226.

47 World Resources Institute, p. 285.

48 World Resources Institute, p. 281.

49 Consumer Reports, "*Wasted Healthcare Dollars*," July 1992, p. 436.

50 Consumer Reports, p. 439.

51 Wright, p. 262.

52 Owen Ullmann and Karen Schneider, "Wealthy will lose, low-income people with jobs will win," *The Times-Picayune* [New Orleans], February 18, 1993, p. A-6, col. 6.

53 Tom Mashberg, "U.S. awakens to debt nightmare," *The Times-Picayune* [New Orleans], November 7, 1992, p. A-1, A-6.

54 Alfred J. Watkins, *Red ink II* (Lanham, Maryland: Hamilton Press, 1988), p. 14.

55 Mashberg, p. A-6.

56 President Clinton's first speech to Congress

57 Mashberg, p. A-1.

Chapter Five—Nuts and Bolts

1 Tax Foundation, *Facts and Figures on Government Finance 1992* (Washington, D.C.: Government Printing Office, 1992), p. 93.

2 John Robbins, "*Realities for the 90's*," excerpted from Diet for a New America (Walpole, New Hampshire: Stillpoint, 1987), p. 6.

3 Lester R. Brown, Christopher Flavin, and Hal Kane, *Vital Signs 1992: The Trends That Are Shaping Our Future* (New York: Norton, 1992), p. 77.

4 Ted Williams, "*The Last Bluefin Hunt*," Audubon July-August 1992, p. 15.

5 Brown, p. 77.

Chapter Six—Three Problems—Diet, Inflation, and Taxes

1 John Robbins, *Diet for a New America* (Walpole, New Hampshire: Stillpoint, 1987), p. 263.

2 Robbins, pp. 250-251.

3 Diane Duston, "Food labels must tell all, stricter U.S. standards say," *The Times-Picayune* [New Orleans], December 3, 1992, p. A-4.

4 John Robbins, (Host), "Diet for a New America Your Health, Your Planet," (*life*guides KCET Video, 1991)

5 United States Department of Health and Human Services, "Facts About Blood Cholesterol," (Washington D.C.: Government Printing Office, October 1990), p. 2.

6 Clarence Wilbur *Taber, Taber's Cyclopedic Medical Dictionary* (14th ed.) (Philadelphia: F. A. Davis, 1981), p. 219.

7 Taber, p. 219.

8 John Merline, "Clinton's New War On Drugs," *Investor's Business Daily* [Los Angelos], February 18, 1993, p. 2, col. 4.

9 Merline, p. 2, col. 5.

10 Merline, p. 2, col. 5.

11 John W. Wright, General Editor, *The Universal Almanac 1991* (Kansas City, Missouri: Andrews and McMeel, 1990), p. 271.

12 Wright, p. 271.

13 Wright, p. 272.

14 Wright, p. 272.

15 World Resources Institute, *Environmental Almanac* (New York: Houghton Mifflin, 1991), p. 66.

16 Wright, p. 276.

17 *World Resources Institute*, p. 67.

18 Wright, p. 274.

19 World Resources Institute, pp. 65-66.

20 World Resources Institute, p. 65.

21 Wright, p. 272.

Chapter Seven—Beyond Arithmetic

1 Morris Kline, *Mathematics: The Loss of Certainty* (New York: Oxford University Press, 1980), pp. 124-126.

2 Dirk J. Struik, *A Concise History of Mathematics* (3rd ed., rev.) (New York: Dover, 1966), pp. 102-103.

3 John Robbins, *Diet for a New America* (Walpole, New Hampshire: Stillpoint, 1987), p. 263.

Chapter Eight—When Linearity Isn't Enough

1 Robert Ornstein and Paul Ehrlich, *New World New Mind: A Brilliantly Original Guide to Changing the Way We Think About the Future* (New York: Simon and Schuster, 1989), pp. 74-75.

2 Theodore Modis, *Predictions* (New York: Simon and Schuster, 1992), p. 17.

3 Modis, p. 63.

4 Modis, p. 64.

5 Modis, p. 242.

6 Modis, pp. 73-74.

Bibliography

Angell, Norman. *The Story of Money*. Garden City, New York: Garden City Publishing Company, Inc., 1929.

Beckmann, Petr. *A History of Pi*. New York: St. Martin's Press 1971.

Boorstin, Daniel J. *The Discoverers*. New York: Vintage, 1985.

Brown, Lester R., Christopher Flavin, and Hal Kane. *Vital Signs 1992: The Trends That Are Shaping Our Future*. New York: Norton, 1992.

Cajori, Florian. "*The Egyptians*," in *Growth of Mathematics: From Counting to Calculus*. ed. Robert W. Marks. New York: Bantam, 1964.

Collins, Gail and Dan Collins. *The Millennium Book*. New York: Doubleday, 1991.

Dantzig, Tobias. *Number: The Language of Science* 4th ed., rev. Garden City, New York: Doubleday, 1954.

Davis, Philip J., and Reuben Hersh. *The Mathematical Experience*. Boston: Houghton Mifflin Company, 1981.

Demko, George J. with Jerome Agel and Eugene Boe. *Why in the World: Adventures in Geography*. New York: Doubleday, 1992.

Durning, Alan. *How Much Is Enough?*. New York: Norton, 1992.

Feltman, John, ed. *Prevention Magazine's Giant Book of Health Facts*. New York: Rodale, 1991.

Ferris, Timothy. *Coming of Age in the Milky Way*. New York: Morrow, 1988.

Flegg, Graham. *Numbers: Their History and Meaning*. London: Andre Deutsch Limited, 1983.

Gamow, George. *One Two Three ... Infinity: Facts and Speculations of Science*. New York: Mentor, 1953.

Glasstone, Samuel. *Sourcebook on the Space Sciences*. Princeton: Van Nostrand, 1965.

Gore, Al. *Earth in the Balance: Ecology and the Human Spirit*. New York: Houghton Mifflin, 1992.

Groseclose, Elgin. *Money and Man: A Survey of Monetary Experience*. New York: Frederick Ungar Publishing Co., 1961.

Kline, Morris. *Mathematics: The Loss of Certainty*. New York: Oxford University Press, 1980.

Kozol, Jonathan. *Savage Inequalities*. New York: Crown, 1991.

Lean, Geoffrey, Don Hinrichsen, and Adam Markham. *Atlas of the Environment*. New York: Prentice Hall Press, 1990.

Lerza, Catherine, and Michael Jacobson. *Food for People, Not for Profit: A Sourcebook on the Food Crisis*. New York: Ballantine, 1975.

Modis, Theodore. *Predictions*. New York: Simon and Schuster, 1992.

Ornstein, Robert and Paul Ehrlich. *New World New Mind: A Brilliantly Original Guide to Changing the Way We Think About the Future*. New York: Simon and Schuster, 1989.

Panati, Charles. *Panati's Extraordinary Endings of Practically Everything and Everybody*. New York: Harper and Row, 1989.

Paulos, John Allen. *Innumeracy: Mathematical Illiteracy and Its Consequences*. New York: Hill and Wang, 1988.

Perlin, John. *A Forest Journey: The Role of Wood in the Development of Civilization*. New York: Norton, 1989.

Richardson, Dennis W. *Evolution of an Electronic Funds Transfer System*. Cambridge, Massachusetts: Colonial Press Inc., 1970.

Robbins, John. *Diet for a New America*. Walpole, New Hampshire: Stillpoint, 1987.

Stewart, Ian. *Game, Set and Math: Enigmas and Conundrums*. London: Penguin, 1991.

Struik, Dirk. *A Concise History of Mathematics*. 3rd. ed., rev. New York: Dover, 1966.

Taber, Clarence Wilbur. *Taber's Cyclopedic Medical Dictionary*. 14th ed. Philadelphia: F. A. Davis, 1981.

Tax Foundation. *Facts and Figures on Government Finance 1992*. Washington, D.C.: Government Printing Office, 1992.

Van Doren, Charles. *A History of Knowledge: The Pivotal Events, People, and Achievements of World History*. New York: Ballantine, 1991.

Wilson, Colin. *New Pathways in Psychology: Maslow and the Post-Freudian Revolution*. New York: Mentor, 1974.

World Resources Institute. *Environmental Almanac*. New York: Houghton Mifflin, 1991.

Wright, John W. gen. ed. *The Universal Almanac 1991*. Kansas City: Andrews and McMeel, 1990.

Index

About the Author

Ira Nirenberg was born in Paterson, New Jersey and was educated in the public school system. He earned his undergraduate degree in Physics from *Rutgers, The State University of New Jersey*, and his Masters Degree in Physics from *Kent State University* in Ohio.

He has worked as an exploration geophysicist, taught math and physics at three universities, published articles on both math and travel and conducted workshops on math and physics for school teachers. He currently teaches gifted students at Benjamin Franklin High School in New Orleans, Louisiana.

He lives in a small shotgun house with his wife Brenda, a *Registered Nurse* and eight cats.

Send *Living With Math* to a friend!

Additional copies of *Living With Math* may be ordered by completing the information below.

Ship to: (*please print or type*)

Name _____

Address _____

City, State, Zip _____

Day Phone # _____

_____ copies of *Living With Math* @ $12.95 ea.: Total $ _____

Postage and handling @ $3.00 per book: Total $ _____

Louisiana residents add 9% tax: Total $ _____

Total amount of check enclosed: Total $ _____

Make check payable to **Pi Press**.

Send to:
Pi Press
P.O. Box 4161
New Orleans, LA 70118-4161

Discounts are available for orders exceeding ten copies. Inquire by writing to the above address.